Dante's *Commedia*

Dante's *Commedia*

ELEMENTS OF STRUCTURE

Charles S. Singleton

(Originally published as Dante Studies 1)

The Johns Hopkins University Press
Baltimore and London

Reprint edition, 1977
Second printing, 1980
The Johns Hopkins University Press, Baltimore, Maryland 21218
The Johns Hopkins Press Ltd., London

Originally published under the title "*Commedia*": *Elements of Structure* by
Harvard University Press, 1954

Library of Congress Catalog Number 77-5267
ISBN 0-8018-2003-0

To the memory of
LUDWIG EDELSTEIN

Wherefore, I too, desiring to furnish something by way of introduction . . . have thought that something concerning the whole work should be premised, that the approach to the part should be easier and more complete.

Dante to Can Grande

Preface

The four essays here brought together touch briefly (though it is hoped, essentially) on four dimensions of meaning which can be seen to make up the substance and special texture of the poetry of the *Divine Comedy*. One might as appropriately speak of "facets" or "aspects" of meaning, were it not that such terms might rather suggest surface reflections and a brilliance dependent upon the way in which the work is (as a jewel) turned for inspection. But what is considered here is not to be seen as lying on the surface. Each is a dimension in depth, reaching to the very core and substance of the poetry, and present (potentially if not actually) along its developing line wherever this may be assayed. Here, in fine, are constants, basic elements of structure. And "elements" indeed has seemed the best term, all things considered.

It must be a mere coincidence that they agree in number with what Dante and his age conceived to be the components of all that lies beneath the circle of the moon—except the soul of man. We may, at any rate, let the remembered exception signal a warning with regard to any such latent suggestion of metaphor. It is the chief and unifying thesis of the pages that follow that Dante's poetry, in the *Divine Comedy*, is a supreme example of "imitation," that his work was deliberately fashioned as an analogue of that great "poem" which is the created universe as the Christian Middle Ages conceived it. But it is not suggested that the poet worked with the "elements" here distinguished as if these were the basic ingredients of some primal matter. These elements are indeed entirely "of the soul." They constitute modes of thought and feeling about the world which a poet was able to embody in an architecture of the spirit which remains unequalled in our history. Allegory and symbolism are both given to this poet, as modes, out of the model which he had ever before him. They are, first of all, (as we shall see) God's ways of writing. And analogy, in turn, is the comprehensive canon of art by which a medieval Christian poet could do his work as the realist he was.

We might, however (and with such correctives in mind) indulge in the metaphor of physical elements just long enough to consider the fourth which will be called the "substance of things seen." And like some early Greek philosopher, seeking the one element from which all the others would derive, we might consider this fourth as such. This, in the poem, is that first literal and historical ingredient of vision on which all else depends. And Dante himself recognized this, of course, in terms of the established doctrine of the four senses. This is the truly basic element, the first miracle of the poem and mainspring of its great power. Yet that which comes first in the order of being may sometimes come last in analysis, lying as it does at the bottom. Perhaps only when it is found there, at the bottom, as the foundation to all the rest, can we best see what the stuff of it is; finding, maybe with no great surprise, that the stuff is faith. Faith, in this instance, raised to the level of poetic vision and that vision of a scope and a quality such as to distinguish its Christian author among all Christians, medieval or modern.

Essays so brief on matters so extensive in a great structure can, of course, make not the merest claim to exhaust the subject. But is it not clear, by now, that whenever our subject is Dante's poetry, we are not apt to do that anyhow?

Acknowledgments

Three of the following four studies and the Appendix were published in periodicals as follows: *Allegory* in the *Kenyon Review*, XIV; *Pattern at the Center* in the *Romanic Review*, XLII; *Substance of Things Seen* in the *Journal of the History of Ideas*, X; Appendix in *Speculum*, XXV.

The kindness of the editors of these journals in permitting the reprinting of these essays is gratefully acknowledged.

All have been somewhat modified, however, and given an accompaniment of notes which they did not then have, in order to become parts of an integral view of a poem's structure.

CONTENTS

Allegory   1

Symbolism   18

The Pattern at the Center   45

The Substance of Things Seen   61

Appendix: Two Kinds of Allegory   84

Allegory

In his *Letter to Can Grande,* where he explains that his poem is "polysemous" and that its subject is twofold, Dante does not point to the allegory of a journey in the *Comedy.* More senses than one and a duality of subject he explains with respect rather to things seen beyond. The subject, he says, taken in the literal sense, is the "state of souls after death"; whereas, allegorically, it is (to reduce his longer statement of it) God's justice as that may be seen in the state of souls after death.

We take him to mean this: the literal subject, so defined, will point beyond itself in the manner that we may in fact see it everywhere doing as we read the poem. Here are Francesca and Paolo, forever without peace, tossed on an infernal storm. This is the simple and literal fact, such is their state after death. But in the literal fact we may behold the justice of God: for their state, which is a punishment, bears witness to its sufficient reason, its justice. The passion of lust is itself such a storm; peace is forever denied it. It is proper, it is just, that the condition of the lustful after death should be the condition of lust itself; even as in Paradise, that the state of those who are in charity should be the very condition of charity. And so everywhere: in the hemisphere of light surrounding the virtuous pagans in Limbo, in the eternal rending and cleaving of schismatics, in the sewn eyelids of the envious, man's just deserts and God's justice are beheld. Nor is this offered as a justification of God's ways to men. Here is no pleading of a case for God. In His will these things are so, and that is our peace if not always theirs.

Thus, in the *Letter* at this point, Dante is attending to a dimension of the poem to all readers most familiar and most prized, its great dimension in height and depth, a vertical scale in which a gaze of centuries turned inward on the human soul has found the way to objectify itself in vision: a vision so organically one that Dante's own division of it into two senses is very much open to question. But such is the discursive mode of his *Letter*. And such at the moment is ours. It was evidently his hope that thus by division his noble patron and others might see his subject, in this respect, more clearly. It is our present hope that his subject, in yet another respect, may likewise be better seen and better understood.

In spite of Dante's own terminology in the *Letter*, we might somewhat help a prevailing and growing critical confusion in these matters if we could agree to call this aspect of the poem, the state of souls after death along with its "other" meaning, symbolism rather than allegory. We may consider that had Dante, like Milton, couched his poem merely in terms of things seen and known under inspiration of the heavenly Muse, with no narrative of a journey to God and with no protagonist moving as our post of observation within the field of vision, we might still have his twofold subject as he explains it in the *Letter*. In this way, for instance, we should see Virgil dwelling with his companions in Limbo in the hemisphere of light, we should see Beatrice sitting beside ancient Rachel in the light of glory. Virgil and Beatrice, in that case, would exemplify the twofold subject as the *Letter* presents it: their particular state after death and man's deserts under God's justice.

But Beatrice does not keep to her seat, nor does Virgil stay in Limbo. And when Beatrice moves and comes to Virgil in

Limbo, she is recognized by him at once for what we are to
know her to be as the poem unfolds:

> O donna di virtú sola per cui
> l'umana specie eccede ogni contento
> di quel ciel c'ha minor li cerchi sui.
>
> *Inferno* II, 76–78.

> O lady of virtue through whom alone mankind arises above
> all that is contained by that heaven which has its circlings least
> [i.e., the sphere of the moon within which all things are tran-
> sitory].

Beatrice had come to dispatch Virgil to rescue her lover from
the slope of the Hill where his way was blocked by the Wolf.
And from assurances already given by Virgil in the first canto,
we know that her role will be to lead her lover from that point
in the upward way beyond which Virgil may not go. But here
Virgil knows her at once as a guide to more than this one man.
She (and she alone) is that lady by means of whom mankind,
l'umana specie, ascends.

Beatrice's role as guide, and hence her meaning, extends beyond any one man's journey to God. She has a role in mankind's journey to God, which must mean a journey here in this
life. Thus already, at the beginning of the poem, in the terms
of her recognition by Virgil, a dual journey in which she has
a part is put before us. A "journey" there, as well as the "state
of souls" there, can point beyond itself.

Here, then, is yet another dimension of the poem which we
meet in the poem at the start. If Dante said little about it in the
Letter, that was probably because he could take it more for
granted than we may; and because to dwell upon allegory in
this aspect would have meant to focus upon a certain wayfarer
at the center of this subject—and it is not praiseworthy, he tells
us elsewhere, to speak of oneself. At a point near the end of
the *Letter,* to be sure, he does refer to those who may carp and
question his going to Paradise. But let these persons, he says,
read certain works of Augustine and Richard of St. Victor and
Bernard (of Clairvaux).[1] We are certainly not inclined to question his going; but if we do read the particular works referred

to, we see at once that they all treat of the possibility of a journey to God even in this life, a journey of the mind and heart, a possibility ideally open to *umana specie*. Without calling it allegory, Dante in the *Letter* is here pointing to the outline of a twofold journey visible in his poem.

Take Virgil. No one, in the poem, announces or declares his role as guide in a twofold journey, as Virgil at once does for Beatrice, yet the poem has ways of pointing to his similar and coöperative role. When, for instance, Virgil must rebuke his charge for lingering too long over the vulgar spat between Maestro Adamo and Sinon, he says:

> e fa ragion ch'io ti sia sempre a lato
> se più avvien che fortuna t'accoglia
> dove sien genti in simigliante piato.
> *Inferno* XXX, 145–147.

And see to it that I be ever at your side if Fortune should bring you again where there are people in any such dispute.

We can hardly take Virgil to mean (or to mean merely) that this is likely to happen again in the journey there. Virgil means, of course, in the journey here, the journey of our life to which Dante must return. It is here that he must make sure, in the future, that Virgil be at his side. Thus Virgil, like Beatrice, has a dual role as guide, in a journey there and in a journey here.

We take note of obvious things. And these, clearly, are touches which, though they point to a journey here, in themselves give no clear idea of what that journey is. They are signals pointing to some scheme doctrinal or philosophical which, were there no more than this given within the poem, would lie quite outside the work. But the poem has not left outside itself the more precise pattern of that journey. It bears it within itself in such a way that when it points to it, it can be pointing to a pattern objective within the structure.

We may observe the manner in which this can happen at that point in *Inferno* when a knotted cord is thrown into the abyss to summon Geryon out of the Eighth Circle: a cord which, we are now told, Dante has been wearing as a girdle:

Io avea una corda intorno cinta
e con essa pensai alcuna volta
prender la lonza alla pelle dipinta.

Inferno XVI, 106–108.

I had a cord about my waist and with it once thought to
catch the leopard with the painted hide.

Plainly we are here referred back to a moment in the opening
scene of the first canto of the poem when this wayfarer, on
the dark slope of the mountain, had met the leopard, first of the
three beasts which had beset his path there. And if we have
come to see (as it may be hoped that by now we have) that the
three beasts represent the three major areas of sin in Hell, we
glimpse a correspondence between the journey through Hell and
the journey as given in that first scene. The leopard is for fraud.
And here now, at precisely the moment when we are entering
the area of fraud in Hell, we are reminded of the moment back
there before the beast. There are other particulars in this con-
nection which could be examined at this point. Let this however
suffice as an instance of the way in which the dual pattern of
a journey can emerge in Hell.

At no point in the whole of the journey beyond this life
are we more unmistakably referred back to the scene in Canto
I *Inferno* than in Canto I *Purgatorio*. Here the wayfarer girds
himself again, here the ascent may finally begin. It is daybreak
and, as the light dawns, a scene comes clear in outline which
returns us by direct reflection to the situation in the first canto
of the poem. We sense at once the striking resemblance. Dom-
inant in both scenes is the outline of a mountain: a mountain
to be climbed, for there, at the summit, in both instances, lies
happiness and peace. At its base and below, in the one scene,
is bitter darkness, a wild wood and the path to Hell; in the
other, there is Hell itself which has but now been left behind.
By a mountain to be ascended the way of a journey is given,
upward or downward as it may be, between the two poles of
light and darkness.

When the poem is unfolded in its entirety and we may stand
back from it for a comprehensive view of these matters, we
realize that the opening scene in Canto I *Inferno* figured and fore-

cast, as well as any single scene might do, the whole configuration of the journey beyond. There is a special reason why we should feel the reflected presence of that first scene most clearly at the beginning of *Purgatorio;* for in *Inferno* I, in the central focus, a mountain rises as it does in *Purgatorio* I, a mountain at whose summit (as we shall know later) lies the first of two goals. The way of Purgatory is in fact central in the whole of the journey beyond, and is so given in the first scene. The other regions, at the extremities of the way, are suggested here rather than given in outline: Paradise by the light above, Hell by the darkness below. Details in the first scene, not well understood at the moment, will reveal their meaning in the developing journey. Thus, at the beginning, the crest of the mountain is lighted by a planet "which leads man aright by whatever way"; and at the summit of the purgatorial mountain, in the journey beyond, it is Beatrice who comes to fulfill the forecast, coming in the figure of a rising sun.

It is, therefore, small wonder that at the beginning of Purgatory we have a sense of return somehow to a place and to a way already familiar. And there are verses here to signal this:

> Noi andavam per lo solingo piano
> com'om che torna alla perduta strada.
> *Purgatorio* I, 118–119.

> We were going over the solitary plain as one who returns to a way that was lost.

* * * * *

If we have not always seen this quite as clearly as we might, it may be because we have had our difficulties with the opening scene of the poem. Things here do seem to stand in a kind of half-light which does not generally prevail in the rest of the work, even in the dimness of Hell. Here at the beginning, things both are and are not what they seem, as Benedetto Croce notes, beginning his reading of the poem.[2] We move in a kind of double vision. Only, in observing the fact, Croce does what the modern reader is too often tempted to do: to put off on Dante his own inability or his own refusal to accustom his eyes to this light, and say rather that Dante at the outset is under

some strain and special labor to get his poem under way. But
the labor and the strain are Croce's and the modern reader's.
The poet is not striving for single vision (as a later Aesthetics
would hold that he ought to be doing if he means to write poetry). The poet is deliberately leading the reader into double
vision, to place him on what he had every right to assume would
be the most familiar of scenes. There is this about that landscape
at the beginning: we may not mark its whereabouts on any map.
And, when we stand at the doorway of Hell and look back to
where we were before, if we ask ourselves where that was, we
know that we may not exactly say. We cannot locate that first
scene. But that is not the important point. The point is that the
scene was designed to locate us. This language of metaphor (for
all the poet could anticipate of his readers) could hardly be
more familiar, nor these figures more worn by use. Here, simply,
is the way of our life. And Augustine's exclamation, centuries
before, over this way of speaking of it, could really have regis-
tered, even in his time, little of the surprise of novelty. Yet it
can help us to sharpen our view:

> To whom shall I tell, how shall I tell, of the weight of cupidity
> how it presses us down that steep abyss and how charity lifts us up
> by Your spirit which moved over the waters? To whom shall I tell
> it? How shall I tell it? For it is in no space-occupying place that we
> sink and out of which we rise again. What could be more like and
> what more unlike? These are affections, these are loves, these are the
> uncleanness of our own spirits that flow down with the weight of
> the cares we are so attached to; and it is Your sanctity that bears us
> upward by our attachment to freedom from these cares: so that we
> lift up our hearts to You where Your spirit moved over the waters
> and we come to supreme peace when our soul has passed beyond
> these waters where there is no standing ground.[3]

We were noting a matter of close correspondence between
the scene at the beginning and that in *Purgatorio* I. There is
more to be observed. When Dante and Virgil have come forth
to see the stars again, we know they stand not only on what
is the lower slope of a mountain, but on what is, by virtue of
the presence of real water there, a shore as well. Ulysses, as the
poem reminds us at this point, had tried to navigate this sea
before and had failed to reach the dry land where Dante and

Virgil stand. Now, in this particular detail of a "shore," we might say, looking back, that correspondence is at least lacking here between the two scenes. But if we do say this, we show either that we are not close readers of a poem or that we are intolerant of a poem's ways. For water on the first scene there is. Looking down from Heaven, Santa Lucia had pointed to it there, as she urged Beatrice to behold the plight of her lover on the dark slope, struggling before the Wolf:

> Beatrice, loda di Dio vera,
>   ché non soccorri quei che t'amò tanto
>   ch'uscí per te della volgare schiera?
>
> Non odi la pièta del suo pianto?
>   Non vedi tu la morte che'l combatte
>   sulla fiumana ove'l mar non ha vanto?
>   *Inferno* II, 103–108.

Beatrice, true praise of God, why do you not help him who loved you so much that he left the common herd? Do you not hear how piteous his cry? Do you not see how death struggles against him there over that river of which the sea has no boast?

The commentators are in some doubt here. Is this *fiumana* Acheron? Or is it a "mere" metaphor? And what does the modifier "over which the sea has no boast" mean? The commentators are having their difficulties with the focus; and a reading course for some of them would be in order, too, in a language of metaphor from St. Augustine to St. Bernard, a language which the poet had thought he could count on to place the reader. No, this is not Acheron (neither is it a "mere" metaphor if Lucia can see this stream and point to it from Heaven). And if the sea has no vaunt over it, that is because this flood does not flow into any sea. Our primer in metaphor would contain a passage from Hugh of St. Victor (d. 1141) on the Ark:

> . . . let us understand that there are two worlds, the visible and the invisible. The visible, of course, is this physical universe which we see with the eyes of our body, and the invisible is the heart of man which we cannot see. And as in the days of Noah the waters of the flood covered the whole earth, and only the ark was borne up by the waters, and not only could it not be covered, but the more the waters rose, the higher it was raised. And now let us understand the

concupiscence of this world that is in the heart of man as waters of the flood; but understand the ark which is lifted above them as the faith of Christ which treads upon transitory pleasure and aspires to eternal goods which are above. For concupiscence of this world is compared to waters because it. flows and glides, and like water flows downward, always seeking the depths... If a man were to enter his own heart he would be able to see how concupiscence always flows downward to those things that are transitory.*

In a sense it might be regretted that somehow a curtain does not fall at the end of Canto II *Inferno* to mark off the first two cantos of the poem for the prologue which they are. Such a marker would serve to point up some fundamental distinctions as to time and place in the poem, distinctions which must be grasped if we are to see the true nature and outline of its allegory. Just there, at that point, some such device would help us to realize that in the prologue scene we are set up on the stage of this life; that on this first stage we may speak of the actor or actors in the first person plural, as "we," even as the poem suggests in its first adjective. This is the way of our life, the life of soul, this is our predicament. It ought to be the scene we know best, the most familiar scene in the world—and in the poem. Here lies the way of our life. The features of it, the things here that we can make out; a hill, a wood, these beasts, all have their existence there where the *fiumana* runs which Lucia sees from Heaven. Where that is, Augustine and Hugh have helped us to see. Here we are in no space-occupying place. Then: curtain—to rise again on the first act of this play, on a scene before the doorway to Hell which is an abyss that is space-occupying and which, on Dante's map, may be located. The change in scene is not only a change in place. Time has changed. For we do not forget that this is a remembered journey (and hence may not really be given in dramatic form). The man who went that way has now returned. His journey was *there* and it was *then*. And time in yet another sense has changed. Of the scene and of the journey in the prologue we might say "our life." Not so beyond the door. The journey beyond is too exceptional an event to bear any but a singular possessive. It was then, and there, and it was his journey. Whereas in the prologue (even though the tense is past) in so far as we might see this as "our" journey, it takes place, as to time, in a kind of "ever-present," with Every-man as actor.

And yet, no sooner have we imagined a curtain at this point than we could wish it away. It might help us with certain essential distinctions. But the poet has not wanted there any such discontinuity as it might suggest. His problem was not Augustine's "how shall I tell of movements of soul in concrete images." His language is already given to the poet and he uses it with full assurance. His problem is to manage to leave this scene, which is not space-occupying, and to attain to that scene which is; to remove a wayfarer from this scene, where he functions in a mode open to a plural "we," on to a scene and a journey where his role is a most singular one. "Our" journey must become "his" journey, "his" must arise out of "our." A literal and very real journey of a living man, a man in a body of flesh and bone, is to be launched forth from a place that does not occupy space. A curtain cannot help, indeed can only defeat. Only a movement within poetic ambiguity at its fullest power could bring about an organic transition in these terms. But this is not all. The journey to the scene of which we may say "then" and "there" and "his" will leave behind it another of which we may speak in terms of "here" and "now" and "our," leave it and yet not lose touch with it. For his journey beyond will remain potentially open to our journey here, between the two there will be a bridge not cut by any divider, an organic tie, a living way back to metaphor.

Even in the prologue, in "our journey," the birth of a literal sense, "his journey," takes place. Not many verses after the first verse of the poem, in fact, we may see this begin to happen. It is part of the necessary work achieved here in ambiguity that even while the prologue scene is locating us, it is launching him:

> Allor fu la paura un poco queta
>   che nel lago del cor m'era durata
>   la notte ch'io passai con tanta pièta.
> E come quei che con lena affannata
>   uscito fuor del pelago alla riva
>   si volge a l'acqua perigliosa e guata,
> così l'animo mio ch'ancor fuggiva

si volse a retro a rimirar lo passo
che non lasciò giammai persona viva.
Poi ch'ei posato un poco il corpo lasso,
ripresi via per la piaggia diserta. . .

Inferno I, 19-29.

Then was the fear somewhat quieted that had prevailed in
the lake of my heart through the night that I had passed so
piteously. And as one who has come from the deep to the shore,
gasping for breath, turns to gaze back at the perilous water, so
my soul which was fleeing yet, turned back to look upon that
pass which never left anyone in life. When I had rested my
tired body a while, I set out once more across the lonely slope
[and/or *shore*].

Coming through the verses preceding the simile we move in
the recognizable terms of the prologue. Here movement is *moto
spiritale* and the simile will further the action as such. With the
pelago of its first term, we may admire the way the figure has
made use of the *lago del cor* just before. And with the *animo*
fleeing and then turning, the comparison is resolved in a mode
commensurate with the prologue scene. Thus my soul, *moto
spiritale*. All is smooth here.

So smooth indeed that we may fail to remark the extraordinary
strategy of the two verses which follow immediately: "When
I had rested my tired body a while." A body here? How is
that? Is this body to be taken as the hill and the other features
on this scene, to be understood as we have learned to understand
those things? Have we begun another metaphor here? Not so.
This body is no metaphor. As it emerges, a curious bifurcation
is taking place. A dual journey is born. The figure that we see
here now, standing in the body on this "shore," is beginning
to move (before we know this) toward a doorway of Hell that
is no metaphor and toward a journey that is likewise no metaphor.

The strategy is subtle. We note that by this figure a *piaggia*
(which means "shore" as well as "slope") is put here, which
later in the opening scene of Purgatory will find its correspondence, as will the act of coming forth from the *pelago* to stand
on a shore. But of that, enough. I would note rather that we
accept this new thing, this body on this scene, because it is
a tired body, even though or perhaps rather because we do not

pause to put the question: how or why would it be tired? If we do, there is clearly only one answer (and if we evade that answer we confess to our inability to face a poet's way of bringing this mysterious incarnation about within the scene). The body is tired from the struggle out of the *pelago!* But the *pelago,* but that water, is not really there on the scene at all, it is only part of a comparison, it is only in the first term of a simile. No matter. This body is tired from the struggle out of that water; and when it moves on across the deserted shore (shore!) it may no longer be recalled or reduced to metaphor. We are moving now beyond a condition imposed by words. If, in the grammar of rhetoric, we had some term to describe this, some term, say, to match a verb *trasumanar* as it later applies to another "going beyond" in Paradiso, we could make good use of it here.

The whole journey beyond exceeds metaphor. It is irreducible to the kind of allegory in which it had its origin. As this figure of a living man, this whole person soul and body, moves through the doorway to Hell, the poem quits the recognizable and familiar double vision in which it began, to come into single and most singular vision, that is, into single journey; to embodied vision, having a substance and a persuasion that could not have been expected from this beginning. There unfolds the line of a literal journey given as real, and it is the body beyond, the flesh brought into these realms of spirit there, that like a catalyst precipitates everywhere the fleshed, the embodied and incarnate. This man's feet on a slope coming down to a river of blood dislodge stones so that a centaur on guard here draws an arrow from his quiver and with it pushes back his beard to utter his amazement. This man must be carried across the river (since it is boiling) on the back of another centaur, for "he is no spirit that can go through the air." Things seen and touched become what living eyes can see and living hands can touch. *Trattando l'ombre come cosa salda.*[5] His foot strikes the frozen face of a sinner stuck fast in the ice of Cocito, his hands pull chunks of hair from the head of another. This Florentine can walk along with another Florentine under a rain of fire and talk (as to tone) as though this were Florence still. By his speech he will be recognized as Florentine by other fellow citizens. His great-

great-grandfather rejoices at his coming. The particular, the individual, the concrete, the fleshed, the incarnate, is everywhere
with the strength of reality and the irreducibility of reality itself. Here is vision truly made flesh. And the possibility of it
arose and was born back there in the prologue. We shall not
exhaust the mystery of it for all our scrutiny.

It is because this is so that we have never before known an
allegory like Dante's allegory. For in this poem, the embodied,
the real and literal, the irreducible journey, "his" journey beyond, will time and again recall that other journey where the
prologue scene placed us, our journey here. And will do this,
not by inviting us to "undo" the journey there, not by permitting
us to see through the event there as if it were not there, not by
washing out the literal; but by a kind of recall more common
in musical structure by which a theme, known in a prelude,
but then left behind, emerges within another theme in its pro-
gressing development. There is no literary allegory to compare
with this. Our references to Bunyan and to the *Romance of
the Rose* have missed the point completely. We have Bunyan,
if you will, in the prologue scene. But beyond the prologue (we
are driven to desperate comparisons) we have Milton. We have,
that is, an action as surely given in terms of the literal and the
historical as Milton's is. These events are what they are, these
things happened—there, then, once in time. Thus we should
have to put Bunyan and Milton together (may we be forgiven
the violence of these deeds hereafter!) to get Dante. But even
this composite would not yet give us Dante's allegory. In order
to have that, Milton's historical sense, at certain appointed places,
would have to open up to Bunyan, recall and reflect *Pilgrim's
Progress* with which we would have begun. We have seen in
the *Comedy* how this does happen. And we see it best there
because we can really see it nowhere else but there, where a
poet has managed these things in organic structure.

* * *

NOWHERE else. But if we are willing to take time to
remember a kind of allegory which we have pretty well for-
gotten, we may be helped to see better how Dante has con-

structed his. This is the allegory of Holy Scripture. We may well feel justified in turning to it. Dante, in the *Letter to Can Grande*, cites from Psalm 113 (Vulgate) the familiar example and offers the accepted view:

> ... for it is one sense which we get through the letter, and another which we get through the thing the letter signifies; and the first is called literal, but the second either allegorical or moral or anagogical. And this mode, for its better manifestation, may be considered in these verses: "When Israel came out of Egypt, and the house of Jacob from a people of strange speech, Judea became his sanctification, Israel his power." Now if we attend to the letter alone, the departure of the children of Israel from Egypt in the time of Moses is presented to us; if the allegory, our redemption wrought by Christ; if the moral sense, the conversion of the soul from the grief and misery of sin to the state of grace; if the anagogical, the departure of the holy soul from the slavery of this corruption to the liberty of eternal glory. And although these mystic senses have each their special denominations, they may all in general be called allegorical, since they differ from the literal and historical. . .

In the *Convivio*, Dante speaks again of this kind of allegory to distinguish it from another which he there calls the "allegory of poets." By the difference between the two we may better see the essential features of scriptural allegory. The radical difference lies in the nature of the literal sense in the one and in the other. The "allegory of poets," which is that of fable, of parable (and hence is also to be found in the Scriptures), is a mode in which the first and literal sense is one devised, fashioned (*fictio* in its original meaning) in order to conceal, and in concealing to convey, a truth. Not so in the other mode, as we may see from the example cited. There the first sense is historical, as Dante says it is, and not "fiction." The children of Israel did depart from Egypt in the time of Moses. Whatever the other senses may be, this first sense abides, stands quite on its own, is not devised "for the sake of." Indeed it was generally recognized that in Holy Scripture the historical sense might at times be the only sense there. These things have been so; they have happened in time. This is the record of them.

If Dante's model for the allegory which he built into his *Comedy* is to be seen here in this conception of scriptural alle-

gory (and I am convinced that it is) then the primary importance of that fact lies not so much in what it says about his
second or mystic sense as in what it says about his first or
literal. For we can readily see that the nature of the literal in
the model can confirm our sense and understanding of the literal
in the *Comedy:* namely, that in the poem, as in the mode of
scriptural allegory, the literal sense is given as an historical
sense standing in its own right, like Milton's, say—Not devised
in order to convey a hidden truth, but given in the focus of
single vision. (Nothing of more importance could happen in
Dante criticism at present than a general recognition of this
fact.)[6]

Then, as we look in the example at the other senses of scriptural allegory, we see how Dante has built here too according
to his model. In Scripture, as we noted, the historical sense, keeping its full force as such, can and does yield another sense. It
may do this, indeed it will do this, intermittently. And note the
nature of the second sense in the model. In the event there, the
Exodus, is signified another event; in the journey there we see
meanings which bring to mind our journey here. All of the
"other" meanings in the example of the Exodus have our journey,
the movement of soul in the way of salvation, in common. Dante
has followed his model closely.

When the other sense is there in Scripture, it is there simply
because intended there by God. Hence, there was general agreement that only God could write in this mode of allegory, wherein the event signified by the words in its turn signifies the
"other" meaning, and only God could use events as words, causing them to point beyond themselves, only He could make the
Exodus there (the real event) signify our journey here. And
this is of course as it should be. The Word of God was given
us for our salvation; it is proper that the events recorded therein
should now and then look to that matter. There is this, moreover, to be said: the Word of God can count on the eye of a
faithful reader who will be reading for his salvation, ever mind-
ful of our journey here while he reads a Psalm of the Exodus.

A poet has not God's power and may not presume to write
as He can. But he may *imitate* God's way of writing. He may

construct a literal historical sense, a journey beyond (it too happens to be an Exodus!) to be, in the make-believe of his poem, as God's literal sense is in His book (and with God's help he will have the power to make it real). And he will make his allegorical or mystic, his other sense, even as God's: a sense concerning our journey, our way of salvation, here in this life. But there would still be a gap to be filled. The poet is at a disadvantage. His work may not assume the reader's attitude that was sure to be brought to God's: the eye of the faithful ever concerned with our journey here. A poet will lay provision as God's word need not do. This the poet will do by so arranging his poem that the reader comes to his literal sense by first passing through the sense that is to be the second and reflected sense; so that our journey here may then be recalled and reflected along the line of a journey there. The poet will provide in a special way; with a prologue, putting the journey to be reflected where, within his poem and organically, he can control the reflection.

Notes

1. See the Letter to Can Grande in *Opere di Dante*, ed. Società Dantesca (Florence, 1921), p. 445: "Et ubi ista invidis non sufficiant, legant Richardum de Sancto Victore in libro De Contemplatione, legant Bernardum in libro De Consideratione, legant Augustinum in libro De Quantitate Anime et non invidebunt." These works are all found in Migne's *Patrologia Latina* (*hereafter referred to as* PL). Two have been translated into English: Augustinus, *De quantitate animae* (*The Measure of the Soul*), Latin text with English translation and notes by F. E. Tourscher (Philadelphia, 1934); St. Bernard, *De consideratione*, trans. George Lewis (Oxford, 1908). On this point one may also consult E. G. Gardner, *Dante and the Mystics* (London, 1913).

2. Benedetto Croce, *La Poesia di Dante* (Bari, 1921; English trans., D. Ainslee, N. Y., 1922), p. 73: "Specialmente il primo canto dá qualche impressione di stento: con quel 'mezzo del cammino' della vita, in cui ci si ritrova in una selva che non è selva, e si vede un colle che non è un colle, e si mira un sole che non è il sole, e s'incontrano tre fiere, che sono e non sono fiere. . ." The aesthetics of Croce shows a radical unwillingness to admit that allegory can be an integral part of "Poetry," and quite ignores, therefore, the true nature of Dante's allegory. As usual, the aesthetician does not go to the work but demands that the work come to him, to be judged on his terms.

3. *Confessions* XIII, 7. I have borrowed the happy translation "space-occupying place" from the Sheed translation of the work (New York, 1943). The original has: "cui dicam? quomodo dicam? neque enim loca sunt, quibus mergimur et emergimus."

4. *De arca Noe morali* I, vi (PL 176, 672.)

5. *Purgatorio* XXI, 136.

6. The importance of the matter has seemed to justify a fuller examination of the distinction of two kinds of allegory (together with more documentary evidence) in an Appendix at the end of this volume.

Symbolism

In introducing his poem to Can Grande, Dante did not use the term at all. He wrote of a twofold subject in the poem, which taken literally, was the "state of souls after death," and which, in its other intention, was "man, as by good or ill deserts, in the exercise of the freedom of his choice, he becomes liable to rewarding or punishing justice." How, then, without his sanction, may we venture to call this aspect of the *Comedy* symbolism? And how may we claim the subject so conceived to be a dimension of the poem distinct from what we have called its allegory?

The answer is that since Dante did so define his subject, we in turn may not refuse to attempt to understand what he meant, or why he looked upon it in that way; and that, in so doing, we find ourselves brought to focus upon what is but one aspect of the poem's structure. For now, by way of the foregoing considerations, we are the better aware of what such a focus upon *the* subject of the poem would exclude from view: namely, the entire dimension of a journey, that event by which it becomes possible for a living man, guided first by a Virgil and then a

Beatrice, to behold "the state of souls after death." To be sure, we readily conceive that there could have been another way: a manner of direct "inspired" vision which would have left out of the poem any outline whatever of a journey. But what a different poem we should have had if Dante had chosen that way! Instead, we have a journey as a chief feature of his great vision of the afterlife and out of the pattern of it a wealth of meaning arises, a dimension of meaning that concerns us and involves us, as we have seen. Dante is Wayfarer and he moves as "I." That "I" is made open to you, to me, to our journey here.

Thus what we have called the allegorical might also be termed the subjective dimension of the poem, this, of the total structure, being that part which brings in a spectator and renders account of the way in which the *seeing* of the state of souls came about. And of this, the subjective side of the poem, the *Letter* had little to say.

As against that side, then, we would observe that what the *Letter* does define as the poem's twofold subject falls entirely within an objective focus: it is not the *seeing*, but the *seen*. And it is here, in this objective dimension of vision where Dante chose to see his "subject," that we may speak of symbolism as distinct from allegory. But that the term itself, so applied, be justified, must depend upon what seems appropriate to us because of subsequent usage, rather than upon Dante's own terminology which did not provide for this distinction.

We may perhaps get our bearings better in the matter of this distinction if we will consider a single brief episode of the poem near the beginning of the *Purgatory*. There we find staged in miniature and in a most vivid and simple way, the essential situation out of which both allegory and symbolism arise in the medieval Christian view.

1.

Dante and Virgil have just reached the shore of the mountain-island of Purgatory and look out over the ocean waters to behold a little boat approach them, propelled and piloted by an angel. These are souls who are being thus ferried to this place.

As they come they are heard to sing in chorus a Psalm of the Exodus, *In exitu Israel de Aegypto*. Then, at once, when they have disembarked, they come up to Virgil and Dante asking the way up the mountain. But Virgil, although he is still Dante's guide, finds himself in Purgatory in a strange new place and must reply that he does not know the way:

> E Virgilio rispuose: "Voi credete
> forse che siamo esperti d'esto loco;
> ma noi siam peregrin come voi siete."
>
> *Purgatorio* II, 61-4.

> And Virgil replied: "You think perhaps that we are familiar with this place; but we are pilgrims, even as you are."

We may note that already by their song of the Exodus the souls who come over the water (as over some "Red Sea") were declaring themselves to be "pilgrims." Virgil now, in his reply to them, is also recognizing this. And he is placing himself and his charge in that same category. It is important to see this, for it becomes an essential part of the meaning of the incident as that now develops.

When they notice by Dante's breathing that he is alive, the souls who have come up to him and Virgil stand back in amazement. And from out of the group comes one who makes as to embrace the living man. This proves to be an old friend of Dante's, a Florentine musician named Casella, but recently deceased. And after a first exchange of greetings between them (ah, the tone of these conversations in the life beyond: "Where have you *been* these past months?" "How do *you* happen to be here?") Dante asks his musician friend to console him with a song of love such as used to quiet all his desires, for he is very tired from his climb to this place. Whereupon Casella intones one of Dante's own lyrics, a canzone known to us as the second of his *Convivio*. But it seems necessary to get the whole of the little incident before our eyes as the poem presents it:

> E io: "Se nuova legge non ti toglie
> memoria o uso a l'amoroso canto,
> che mi solea quetar tutte mie voglie,
> di ciò ti piaccia consolare alquanto
> l'anima mia, che, con la mia persona

venendo qu., è affannata tanto!"
'*Amor che ne la mente mi ragiona*'
    cominciò elli allor sì dolcemente,
    che la dolcezza ancor dentro mi suona.
Lo mio maestro e io e quella gente
    ch'eran con lui parevan sì contenti,
    come a nessun toccasse altro la mente.
Noi eravam tutti fissi e attenti
    a le sue note; ed ecco il veglio onesto
    gridando: "Che è ciò, spiriti lenti?
qual negligenza, quale stare è questo?
    correte al monte a spogliarvi lo scoglio
    ch'esser non lascia a voi Dio manifesto."
Come quando, cogliendo biada o loglio,
    li colombi adunati a la pastura,
    queti, sanza mostrar l'usato orgoglio,
se cosa appare ond'elli abbian paura,
    subitamente lasciano star l'esca,
    perch'assaliti son da maggior cura;
così vid'io quella masnada fresca
    lasciar lo canto, e gire inver la costa,
    com'uom che va, nè sa dove riesca:
nè la nostra partita fu men tosta.

                            Purgatorio II, 106–133.

And I: "If a new law takes not from you remembrance or
practice of those songs of love that used to quiet all my desires,
may it please you therewith somewhat to console my spirit,
which, coming here with my body, is so wearied." "*Love which
discourses in my mind*," he then began so sweetly, that the
sweetness still sounds within me. My master and I and those
souls who were with him seemed so content as if nothing else
touched the mind of anyone. We were all fast and attentive to
his song, and lo! the venerable old man shouting: "What is this,
tardy spirits! What negligence, what loitering is this? Hasten to
the mountain to put off the slough which lets not God be manifest to you!" As when in picking grain or tares, doves are
gathered at feeding, quiet, without displaying their wonted
pride, if something appears of which they are frightened, they
suddenly leave the food, because assailed by a greater care; so
saw I that newly arrived troupe leave the singing and go toward
the slope, as one goes who knows not where he will come out;
nor was our departure any less sudden.

The *veglio* who comes up shouting this stern injunction to
the group is Cato, met in the preceding first canto of *Purgatory*

as the guardian of this second realm where liberty is won, where the will which had grown crooked in the world is again made straight and free, where "the old man is put off and the new put on," as his words to these pilgrims would declare with their figure of the skin which the snake sheds in the season of hope.

Since the *Comedy* is allegorical and since the events of the journey there can be seen to reflect our journey here, we are invited to consider this incident as if it took place in this life. It is precisely in this regard that the role of pilgrim in which the actors in the scene before us have been cast becomes most significant. This in itself is a way of opening up to allegory. For it is in the figure of those pilgrims there that we are asked to find ourselves and our true condition as Christians. We, even as they, are involved in a journey. And we know by how many passages in Scripture that journey is to be seen as a pilgrimage; the major source of the familiar conception being, no doubt, that chapter of Hebrews beginning with what Dante recognized to be *the* definition of faith—"Now faith is the substance of things hoped for, the evidence of the things not seen"—reviewing the patriarchs from Abel to Abraham to whom the faith had been given, coming, then, to speak thus of them all:

> These all died in the faith, not having received the promises, but having seen them afar off, and were persuaded of them, and embraced them and confessed that they were strangers and pilgrims on earth. For they that say such things declare plainly that they seek a country. And truly, if they had been mindful of that country from whence they came out, they might have had opportunity to have returned. But now they desire a better country, that is, an heavenly: wherefore God is not ashamed to be called their God: for he hath prepared for them a city.[1]

To the reader who has grasped the whole conceptual structure of the *Purgatorio*, the relevance of that passage is most evident. At the ultimate summit of the journey now begun by these souls who have just landed here lies a city prepared for them, an heavenly one, which they all desire. And ahead in the journey for the living man lie two goals: a "city of justice restored" at the top of the mountain, and the heavenly city of the Empyrean.

Keynote now in this new realm is hope in the promise, and movement in faith.

The song of the Exodus, moreover, could not more clearly have pointed to that relevance. These souls have now left Egypt (which is the world, says Augustine)[2] behind them. And the words which Virgil speaks to them place him and Dante within the figure: "We are pilgrims even as you are." It may be observed, moreover, that nowhere in the journey through Hell had the poem suggested that Dante and Virgil were pilgrims. This in itself is the more remarkable in a poem whose very structure of journey rests upon that motif. It is only here where Virgil must declare himself to be a stranger that the wayfarers become pilgrims. This is a "Christian" place, as Hell is not. Here in Purgatory as nowhere else the essential condition of the Christian pilgrim can be reflected; for here even the souls are wayfarers. And a tercet of the second canto of *Purgatorio*, in saying how Dante and Virgil stand now on the shore of this new realm, is deliberately pointing to that very inner state of mind of the Christian which makes him a pilgrim:

> Noi eravam lunghesso mare ancora,
>   come gente che pensa a suo cammino,
>   che va col cuore e col corpo dimora.
>
> *Purgatorio* II, 10-12.

> We were still beside the sea as persons who think of the way ahead, who go in their heart and in their body stay.

We, the living, are obliged to abide yet a while in this life. Nonetheless, our hearts will ever be moving out and upwards on a journey toward a promised land. The unquiet heart of the Christian must ever be ours: "For Thou didst make us for Thee, and unquiet is our heart until it rest in Thee."[3]

All of which considerations prove to be most pertinent as we witness these souls and this living man become so entirely absorbed in Casella's song. For we must consider that if there were but the one literal sense here, much of the meaning would be gone. Taken literally, as simply an incident in Purgatory, there is nothing especially surprising in Cato's coming to scatter these "tardy" souls and send them on their proper way. They are here of course to purge themselves, to become ready to rise to the final beatitude, even as Dante is come here to press on to that same goal. But if what happens there is seen to reflect what might happen in our life's journey, then evidently a new aspect of meaning enters in. And we may put the question which then comes to mind: taken as a happening in this life, what are the implications of the incident? Here, let us say, is a group of listeners (and since what Casella sings is a poem we might also say *readers*) than which no artist or poet could wish for better. Are they not doing what we hope all may do who would enjoy a work of art? Are they not doing the very thing they ought to do in becoming thus completely attentive to that work "as if nothing else touched their mind"? Should they not find, as Dante says to Casella, that all desire is quieted here? In short, may they not be permitted to have that experience of a work of art which modern criticism and aesthetics speak of as a "focus of repose,"[4] or the "terminal" or "intransitive" experience? By what right then does old Cato come up (in this life) with his cry that this is wrong? And how is it that the conscience of all will thereupon acknowledge that Cato is right?

The answer is readily at hand, of course, when we have remembered (and Cato's cry reminds us) that in this life it is our proper condition as Christians to be as pilgrims. And our thought turns to that distinction which Augustine had made between using and enjoying things:

> For to enjoy a thing is to rest with satisfaction in it for its own sake. To use, on the other hand, is to employ whatever means are at one's disposal to obtain what one desires, if it is a proper object of desire; for an unlawful use ought rather to be called an abuse. Suppose, then, we were wanderers in a strange country, and could not live happily away from our fatherland, and that we felt wretched in our wanderings, and wishing to put an end to our misery, determined to return home. We find, however, that we must make use of some mode of conveyance, either by land or water, in order to reach that fatherland where our enjoyment is to commence. But the beauty of the country through which we pass, and the very pleasure of the motion, charm our hearts, and turning these things which we ought to use into objects of enjoyment, we become unwilling to hasten the end of our journey, and becoming engrossed in a fac-

titious delight, our thoughts are diverted from that home whose delights would make us truly happy. Such is a picture of our condition in this life of mortality. We have wandered far from God; and if we wish to return to our Father's home, this world must be used, not enjoyed, so that the invisible things of God may be clearly seen, being understood by the things that are made [Romans 1, 20]— that is, that by means of what is material and temporary we may lay hold upon that which is spiritual and eternal.[5]

Perhaps nowhere more clearly than in this little episode of *Purgatory* can we witness the situation of the work of art within the medieval Christian frame. Moreover, it is evident that the total implications extend beyond the work of art merely, to embrace all things of this life, as Augustine has claimed. In fact, through the broadest implications of the incident, we touch not only upon the essential foundation of medieval allegory and medieval symbolism in art, but on their common foundation in the real world as well—the world which art reflects.

By way of the use which things in this world are thus conceived to have for us, it was common enough to regard the created universe as a book written by God for man to read. Hugh of St. Victor, whom we have already heard on the subject of allegory, may be taken to present the metaphor in the typical way:

For this whole visible world is as a book written by the finger of God, that is, created by divine power; and individual creatures are as figures therein not devised by human will but instituted by divine authority to show forth the wisdom of the invisible things of God. But just as some illiterate man who sees an open book looks at the figures but does not recognize the letters: just so the foolish natural man who does not perceive the things of God sees outwardly in these visible creatures the appearances but does not inwardly understand the reason. But he who is spiritual and can judge all things, while he considers outwardly the beauty of the work inwardly conceives how marvelous is the wisdom of the Creator.[6]

The book of the universe is in this way *twofold*. Hugh has in mind that same text which Augustine cited and which is so fundamental to all conceptions of symbolism in the Middle Ages: "For the invisible things of Him from the creation of the world are clearly seen, being understood by the things that are made, even His eternal power and godhead."[7]

Again, for the sake of yet another example, we may find in Saint Bonaventura's *Breviloquium* this same notion of a twofold book:

> . . . the First Source made this visible world to declare Himself, namely, so that man, through it as by a mirror and by traces (*speculum et vestigium*) might be brought to love and praise God the author. And accordingly the book is twofold (*duplex*): one, that is, written within, which is the eternal art and wisdom of God; and the other written without, that is, the visible world.[8]

Because the world could thus be viewed as a book written *digito Dei* and by nature *duplex;* and, moreover, because Holy Scripture (without metaphor) is also properly called the book of God; it becomes possible and indeed common to speak, within the medieval view, of two books written by God,[9] each exhibiting a literal and an "other" sense. In Holy Scripture, as we have seen, it is the event, such as the Exodus, which is conceived to point beyond itself to another event, our salvation through Christ; whereas in the "Scripture" of a created universe, things made by God point beyond themselves to the invisible things of their Maker, to His art and wisdom and power. It is important to note that both "books" are written by God for our salvation. This is obvious enough in the case of Holy Scripture. But it is also true of the other "book," though we are far less accustomed to any such view—the less so, since it was one of the first concerns of modern science, as it arose in Renaissance times, to get this kind of symbolism out of nature. Modern science had to reëstablish and justify a curiosity in things for their own sake, a terminal value in things, and this it had fully achieved in a Galileo, for one, whose eye could follow the pendulum movement of chandeliers in churches "as if nothing else touched his mind," and formulate a mathematical analysis of the phenomenon. To get a sense of the distance which separates his attitude from that by which the world of nature became a book, we might recall yet another page from the *Confessions* where Augustine pronounces judgment upon idle curiosity, finding it so rife in himself:

> Notwithstanding, in how many petty and contemptible trifles is this curiosity of ours daily tempted: and how often we do slip that

way, who is able to recount? How often when people tell vain
stories do we at first bear with them, as it were, for fear of giving
offence to the weak; and yet by degrees, by and by we willingly
give ear to them? I no longer go to the Games to see a dog chasing
a hare, but if in going through a field I come upon the same thing,
that chase may easily draw me off from some serious thought and
draw me after it, not turning me out of the road with the body of
my horse, but yet with the inclination of my heart: yea, and didst
not Thou, by making me see my infirmity, quickly admonish me,
either through the sight itself by some contemplation to raise myself
toward Thee, or wholly to despise and pass it by; I should stand
gaping at it. What shall I say, whenas sitting in mine own house, a
lizard catching flies, or a spider entangling them in her nets often
makes me attentive to them. These are small creatures but is it not
the same thing? I proceed indeed to praise thee the wonderful Creator and Disposer of all: but that is not the occasion of my beginning to be attentive to them.[10]

Whenever it happens that the things of nature are seen as
things only, when the eye rests upon them as terminus, then the
religious conscience of the centuries which reach from Augustine
to Dante will cry out that something is very wrong. For things
are not things merely. Things in the created universe are both
things and signs. In the realm of appearance man's eye should
ever discern the invisible things of God. But suppose things *do*
cease to point beyond themselves and do not yield an "other"
meaning? Where then does the trouble lie? With the spectator,
Augustine would say, first of all. For it is when our heart grows
quiet, making its peace with this world, that this can happen;
it is when we forget that we are pilgrims.

We touch here on the common root of both allegory and
symbolism in the medieval Christian frame. Supporting them
both is that unquiet heart of the Christian pilgrim. Thus God's
two books, both written for our salvation, point us along the
way of our journey: the one, Holy Scripture, in which events
(such as the Exodus) yield the very sense of our journey, the
other, the created universe, in which things bespeak the invisible
things of the Divine Architect, directing the inclination of our
minds and hearts to Him.

But in finding the common source of both allegory and symbolism thus to be the unquiet heart of the Christian pilgrim,

we must beware of reducing them to mere subjective phenomena. Most readily do we conceive that such a view as Augustine's represents a kind of projection of man's concern for salvation into the field of vision, whether that be Scriptural history or nature. Since the Renaissance, and, shall we say, since Kant,[11] we are especially ready to do this. It was therefore something of a hard saying for our modern mind that, in the case of the Exodus, God had used an episode of real history as an author can use a word, causing it to speak of our salvation through Christ. Yet such is the conception of scriptural allegory and, we recall, when he repeats the accepted definition, such is Dante's claim: ". . . for it is one sense which we get through the letter, and another which we get *through the thing which the letter signifies*." [Italics mine.]

Likewise, in the dimension of symbolism, it is quite as hard for us to grant that the sign which is found in things inheres in them objectively. Again we are too much of the Renaissance and live too much with its consequences to conceive of this without some effort. Yet for Augustine and Dante we may be sure that the sign is thought to be in the thing and yielded by the thing. God had put it there. Man does not contribute it out of his own mind and heart. He discovers it. And this, among all our general considerations of the structure of Dante's *Comedy*, is most important. Unless, by an effort of the imagination we can again achieve this view, then we may not hope to be adequate readers of the *Divine Comedy*, but shall be forever recasting Dante and his world into the image of our own.

The song which Casella sang and which those pilgrims in Purgatory became so absorbed in, is just that, a song, and not an object in nature. Yet we can allow in its place such an object, a hare pursued by a hound across a field, let us say, or a spider spinning her web. Then, *mutatis mutandis*, if we become absorbed in that thing as did these pilgrims in Casella's song, Cato can still come rushing up to us with that same shout, and conscience can still proclaim in us that Cato is right. Things are to be used, not rested in. No object in the pilgrim's field of vision may properly have terminal value in itself. This is the claim of the medieval Christian conscience, and this claim is the whole basis of medieval symbolism. The object may not be terminal, for God intended that He alone should be so, where man is the traveler. Ontology rests upon His intentions, and the real world which he created *ex nihilo* is grounded there for support.

We may turn back from these considerations to Dante's claim in the *Letter* for his twofold subject. The focus, as he there states the matter, is upon things seen; "the state of souls after death." But we must at once acknowledge that things seen in the fiction of this poem are no part of the world of nature which we the living behold. Instead, they are situated on the scene of the afterlife. Might not a poet have chosen to consider things seen there, on that extraordinary otherworldly ground, to be sufficient in their mere visual or presentational aspect? Yet Dante did not choose to behold them that way, nor as poet to present them so. What it is important for us to see is this: it is merely part of the realism of Dante's vision that the things which are seen on the stage of the afterlife are as the things which we see on the stage of this world. Thus, in the world beyond, even as in this world (when man's eye is not purblind), things seen will point beyond themselves to the invisible things of God. In eschatological space also, things are both things and signs. That is, to transpose to Dante's terms in the *Letter*, a state of souls after death will yield an "other" sense; for that state is either one of reward or of punishment, and rewards and punishments are from God and manifest His justice. This is that dimension of the *Comedy* which we shall do well to distinguish from allegory, because the models, as we can see, are in fact distinct in their reality and by their nature: symbolism is Dante's imitation of the structure of the real world, and allegory is his imitation of the structure of God's other book, Holy Scripture. If we will but look upon the world as he conceived it, we shall see that the art of this religious poet is essentially realism.

2.

Each particular state after death discloses by certain intelligible signs its justness as a punishment or a reward. In that justness God's justice is witnessed, His might and wisdom and art. At times it is in these terms that, as he confronts the awesome spectacle in the world beyond, the poet will break off his narrative to exclaim:

> O somma sapienza, quanta è l'arte
> che mostri in cielo, in terra e nel mal mondo,
> e quanto giusto tua virtù comparte!
>
> *Inferno* XIX, 10–13.

O highest Wisdom, how great is the art which Thou dost show in the heavens, on earth and in the evil world! And how justly doth Thy power apportion!

Here is precisely the focus in which we look for what can be given by the signs which are in things, and we might easily take the words to be directed upon any one of the multitude of scenes which reach, one after the other, the long way of this journey to God. Hence it can be nothing but the merest arbitrary choice that will take one rather than another of those scenes as representative of the symbolism of God's justice as we meet it throughout the whole of the poem. Moreover, the way in which the signs of justice present themselves in any given scene will ever display a variety which defies simple formulation. The poet's work was not done by preconceived formula mechanically applied. Each scene arises from its own real center of inspiration, nor in a single instance do we feel that the poet is near the risk of repetition. That "the individual is ineffable" may well be a dictum generally valid for our commoner powers of expression, but it does not hold for this poet. His vision attains to the concrete and the living. The variety of beings and states of being which arise before the eye of his reader acknowledges only such limits as the design of one hundred cantos can itself impose. It is to the greater glory of the poem that our own willful purposes of abstractive analysis are quite defeated in this regard.

However, with an eye in particular upon the matter of the ways in which things seen are caused to yield their signs, we may at least take note of a considerable range in levels of communication throughout the poem's symbolism. Of course, here without any doubt, the peculiar limitations of a modern reader do enter in. What to him may seem most recondite may easily have been far less so to Dante's contemporary reader; and what we might take to be a varying depth in the poem in this regard could be merely the symptoms of a varying distance at which we find ourselves from this or that aspect of culture or mode of thought and feeling of the poet's age.

And yet, with due allowance for all this, it is nonetheless evident that we may with some reason speak of a varying depth in the level at which justice is symbolized, if we review the whole course of the poem.

Here at one extreme, for example, are the soothsayers of Malebolge, their heads twisted about on their bodies, obliged to walk backwards in order to see their way. Doubtless any reader will feel that the justice of this punishment is obvious enough. Yet the poet has not hesitated to make an explicit declaration of it in the canto, having Virgil point to one of these sinners to say:

> Mira c'ha fatto petto de le spalle:
> perchè volle veder troppo davante,
> di retro guarda e fa retroso calle.
>
> *Inferno* XX, 37–40.

> See how he has made a chest of his back; because he sought to see too far ahead, he looks backwards and makes a backward way.

And this single instance of justice declared will remind any reader who knows the poem of many another. There in the ninth ditch of Malebolge, for yet another example, are the sowers of scandal and schism, forever butchered anew in their eternal rounds by the sword of a devil. Here, heresiarchs among others declare themselves and once more we may well feel that it wants no rare acumen to perceive that in their cleavage is symbolized that which they wrought within the Church which is Christ's body. Yet one of them will point deliberately to the justice of it:

> E tutti li altri che tu vedi qui,
> seminator di scandalo e di scisma
> fur vivi, e però son fessi così.
>
> *Inferno* XXVIII, 34–37.

> And all the others whom you see here were sowers of scandal and schism when alive, and for that reason are cleft so.

It is among these souls that we meet the unforgettable Bertram de Born, punished for setting a son against his royal father, carrying his severed head by the hair, dangling like a lantern; and his words proclaiming the reason for this his state after death are these:

> Perch'io partì' così giunte persone,
> partito porto il mio cerebro, lasso!
> dal suo principio ch'è in questo troncone.
> Così s'osserva in me lo contrapasso."
>
> *Inferno* XXVIII, 139–142.

Because I disjoined persons so united, I carry my brain disjoined, alas, from its main stem which is in this trunk. Thus is retribution observed in me.

In the method of justice, generally, *"contrapasso"* [12] appears in one way or another to prevail as a guiding principle. And it is because of this that the justice of a given punishment must reflect a conception of the nature of the sin involved.

Hence, at one extreme we recognize that we meet often enough in the circles of Hell and on the terraces of Purgatory this kind of symbolizing at the surface level. Here the sign, already evident in itself, is made the more so by overt pronouncement. But we must also recognize that we encounter symbolism in the poem at a level far more subterranean and complex. The punishment of Satan will serve as a fair example. And to get that before us in all significant detail, we shall have to enter into the concrete and most allusive texture of the verses which present him in his punishment.

In fact it would probably be somewhat instructive in this instance to keep an eye upon ourselves as reader, and observe by what way we come to see what the poet has wanted us to see in the symbolism of justice at this its more hidden level. By attending to the reader's experience as such, as well as to the poem, in this matter of symbolism, we may better take stock of what the particular demands upon the reader of the *Comedy* are at such not infrequent moments as this; what the terms are on which full communication is possible—a test case, in short. And in order that it may be in keeping with Dante's particular view of a twofold subject, let us recall Hugh of St. Victor's remarks (which Dante would have understood so well) about the two kinds of readers who may be imagined to look upon the "twofold book."[13] Hugh spoke of a "natural" reader, on the one hand, who would take in the scene merely in its physical and visual aspect, and of another "spiritual" reader, who would see not only all that the natural reader sees, but would also understand the reasons that lie within. It is he, in fine, who can read the things as signs.

Turning, then, to the example of Satan's punishment, let us imagine that we come first to this final scene of *Inferno* in the role of Hugh's first reader, seeing with him only what meets the eye here as spectacle.

Gradually the Demon is seen towering in the darkness above the ice which holds him fast as in a vise at this center of the material world. A cold wind blows from him, stirred by three pairs of huge batlike wings which are seen to grow out of the base of the monster's three heads. In each of his three mouths a sinner is chewed eternally, and these three so punished, our spectator is told, are Judas, Brutus and Cassius. Impressively enough, the three faces of this colossus are colored, each with a distinct hue of its own: the middle face being red, the others yellow and black respectively.

Such are the essential features of the figure as discerned by our natural reader's eye. We are granting all the while, of course, the poet's power to make the scene as vivid as he in fact does make it. But admitting this, we must recognize that we reach here the limits of what this first reader could take in. He sees. He does not understand.

If now we bring to the scene that other of Hugh's readers who sees both the outward aspect and understands the "reason" within, what shall be the first awareness permitted him? That ought perhaps to be the knowledge of what this creature was before he fell to this condition. A verse in the poem provides a reminder, looking upon the demon as *la creatura ch'ebbe il bel sembiante*, (*Inferno* XXXIV, 18; "the creature who was once so beautiful")— and never did the past absolute tense in Italian have more of its special force than here! Our knowledgeable reader is thus aware that Satan, before he fell to this condition, was the brightest of all the angels and was, of course, of the highest order, the Seraphim. Let us also grant him the knowledge that Isaiah by prophetic vision had had,[14] that Seraphim have six wings. In this way at least one detail in the scene finds its reason: Satan still has the wings he had, though they are not as they were, but grow now at the base of three heads which before his fall he certainly did not have.

These three heads of Satan, in fact, a detail which our natural reader took in but did not understand, demand a reason with this our other reader. And here we do well to watch our test case closely. How is this reader to come to see the reason here? Clearly we are gradually allowing him more and more knowledge, in order that he may see more. Thus we proceed to grant him the further awareness that Satan's sin was one of pride, indeed the supreme instance of that sin. And we note that a tercet of the poem at this point reflects upon the justice of Satan's present state as a just consequence of that sinful act:

> S'el fu sì bello com'elli è or brutto,
>   e contra'l suo fattore alzò le ciglia,
>   ben dee da lui proceder ogni lutto.
>
> Inferno XXXIV, 34-37.

If he was once as beautiful as he is now ugly, and raised his eyes against his Maker, well must all woe proceed from him.

To this extent, at least, the reasons for the particular form of justice are here declared.

But if our hypothetical reader is to see further in this matter, he must be allowed more knowledge yet: not only an awareness of the category of Satan's sin but also of its special nature. He must know what Satan willed, what Satan intended, in that upsoaring moment of pride by which he fell. *Satan aspired to be as God.* Note that we have only to grant this awareness and there comes at once a total illumination in understanding which gathers in the scattered details of the scene as expressive parts of a whole. Now our spiritual reader sees as he desires to see. That is, he understands. Yet no voice within the poem declares this particular point to him, nowhere is this controlling idea brought to the surface in overt declaration. How then is our reader expected to come by it? Evidently he must bring the idea to the scene. It must be part of his equipment as reader. The poet is counting on that. Of course it is not really so very much to expect of a

Christian reader. The idea is given by Scripture, by theology, by Christian doctrine.[15]

We take stock of obvious things and in their simplest terms. The case of this imagined reader is a test case for us. We stand to learn from it something essential, though obvious, about reading the poem.

Now the "invisible things" of justice are clearly discerned. Satan aspired to be as God, and the justice of his punishment is that now he is what he aspired to be. He is in fact like God—a grotesque monstrous counterpart of the triune Godhead. Details fall easily into place. The three heads, first of all. Satan's aspiration has become a reality. What a triune Godhead he is indeed! We take note of a further detail which only now can disclose its meaning: Satan's three heads are joined at the top—unity in trinity. And what of the color of the faces? Is there symbolic meaning here as well?

For the moment, this might be as far as we would choose to imagine our "other" reader going in his progressive understanding of the reasons for the particular form of Satan's punishment. In a sense, this is far enough anyway. To reason's eye the justice of the punishment is now apparent. It was quite enough to know the special nature of Satan's sinful intention to begin to see the justness of "*contrapasso*" in his case. Until he had looked through that idea, even the second reader had no significant advantage over his "natural" confrere who could see but could not understand.

We noted along the way, to be sure, how the poem was here and there helping the reader to understand by way of references and turns of phrase. To that extent the imagined test was not strictly that of a spectator confronting a mute spectacle, without benefit of promptings from any quarter. For all the while the spectacle was being put before the eye, the poem was bringing in verbal reminders. But even so, such special references could not have been taken in as meaningful in themselves without that certain awareness which our second reader had to bring to the poem from without.

A single verse here can make its own signal contribution. Indeed it is by way of this verse that we first begin to look directly at Satan: *lo'mperador del doloroso regno*.[16] Satan the "emperor." There were other such references to him along the way. We have, in fact, come toward him through Inferno as toward one who resides in the innermost citadel of a fortified city. But it is only when we can hold the entire poem before our mind's eye that we can grasp the full implications and see that around this idea of "emperor" a balance in the whole poem is built. This progressive penetration of a journey through Inferno toward a center is, we see in the end, clearly counterbalanced in the realms of Paradiso. Each center has its emperor: in Heaven, He who is pure spirit; in Hell, this monster, grotesque image of the Other, fixed in the ice of his own making. Thus the image of Satan has symbolic meaning not merely within the frame of a particular creature's punishment, but as part of the order and symmetry of the whole cosmic plan.

But we left our second "spiritual" spectator confronting the detail of the colored faces of Satan. What can he be expected to make of this? As spectator merely, probably nothing of which he can feel very certain. The only established color symbolism which comes to his mind is that of the three theological virtues, faith, hope and charity, whose colors are most familiar as white and green and red. Would these colors of the faces of Lucifer, black, yellow and red, be signifying in some way some corresponding or negating symbolism?

It is here that it becomes necessary to imagine our second spectator not as spectator only, but as reader—and a very attentive reader at that. We permit him now to confront not a scene merely which some painter might have set before him, but the poem itself in its immediate and most intimate verbal texture. He must now see as reader, and words themselves must do the work of visual detail and yield the sign.

Relaunched along the line of the poem in this way, he will begin at once to find other "traces" by which meaning is disclosed. Indeed the opening verse of this last canto of Inferno may now begin in itself to suggest a significance which would have remained quite hidden to that "natural" reader who brought to the poem only an innocent if impressionable eye.

Vexilla regis prodeunt inferni

This verse, our discerning reader must be permitted to know, is (except for the addition of its last word) the first verse of a hymn [17] appointed, in the Roman breviary, to be sung at vespers on the Saturday before Passion Sunday. Most appropriately, then, does it come in here, since within the fiction of the poem that is precisely the time when these two wayfarers have arrived at Satan.

The first verse of this familiar hymn would be quite enough, we may further allow, to suggest the rest:

> Vexilla regis prodeunt
> fulget crucis mysterium
> quo carne carnis conditor
> suspensus est patibulo.

The banners of the king come forth, the mystery of the Cross shines forth, where He in flesh, who made our flesh, hangs upon the gibbet.

As this first stanza of the hymn can alone suggest, and as full knowledge of the original occasion of the composition of the work and its consequent use in the services of the Church would certainly make clear, Fortunatus' poem is a processional hymn in honor of the Holy Cross. What it proclaims as ritual and mystery was, on the occasion of its first use, literal fact. Forth come the banners of the king, and the king is Christ. Eyes are directed by the verses to see His Cross where it comes with its Holy Victim upon it. "*Arbor decora et fulgida*," says another verse, whereby the *patibulum* of the first stanza is envisaged as such a tree.

By the light of even these details our attentive reader can see a function of that initial verse in Latin. Clearly it is designed to guide his attention into a particular focus upon what is now to come. The banners of the king of Hell—but is this a procession? Shall we expect to see a Cross with a Holy Victim upon it here? We peer into the darkness trying to see by the light of this suggestion. At first it is not a cross at all that is discerned, but something much more like a windmill. Then when we are nearer, we see: the figure is indeed somewhat like a cross. That upright body with the two heads on either side of a central one appears as something not unlike the outline of a *patibulum* as originally conceived.[18] And here upon this "cross" are victims: three such, punished by the grinding teeth of those huge mouths. And at the center where, if this were the scene on Golgotha, Christ as victim would have been, there is Judas.

But the verse of the hymn has suggested not only a Cross. It gave us to expect a procession. Yet this infernal "cross" has not only not come forward, as in the procession heralded by the hymn; instead this "cross" in Hell is forever fixed where it is. There is irony in the fact, as there is irony in the opening proclamation of a "king's" banners. And that irony is also an aspect of the justice.

So much can that initial verse in Latin contribute to the symbolic import of this scene, for a reader in whom it can awaken the intended associations. But there is more. The notion of *procession* which the hymn so clearly brings to the fore can lead to a notable increase in meaning by association from out of yet another quarter, if we will but reëstablish contact with that central illuminating idea noted before.

Satan aspired to be as God. And ironically he has his wish. His three heads joined at the top are the token of that. But what knowledge of the Triune Original does our reader bring to his reading at this point? Is it too much to expect him to come with some of the fundamental concepts of Christian theology? Dante, we venture to surmise, did not think this too great an expectation; for he has deliberately woven into the verses by which we approach Satan two signals which can have meaning only for a reader who brings those certain concepts to his reading of the poem at this point.

Before examining these notions and ending a little experiment in the reading of symbolism, let it be recalled that we have allowed our spectator to become reader and have turned from the kind of purely visual symbolism which a painter might use (such as the detail of the three heads of Satan) to the kind of verbal sign which belongs uniquely to poetry. The symbolism of the *Comedy* functions by way of both kinds of signs. But it is the sign in the verbal order of the kind now to be noted that contributes to the concrete texture of the poem so much of its special depth and richness of meaning.

It is Satan's punishment to be as God; and thus the knowledge which is the special province of theology becomes at this point especially relevant. For only by knowing how the true triune God is, may we see how triune Satan images the counterpart.

We need, in particular, to know that theology considers that between the persons of the Trinity there are two fundamental relations traditionally denoted by the special terms of "procession" and "spiration." Now, we have seen that the notion of procession was given by the opening verse of the hymn. The presence of this notion is further confirmed a few verses later by the corresponding verb in the infinitive: *ben dee da lui proceder ogni lutto.*

But note too that the rhyme word of the second tercet of the canto is contributing at once the companion notion of "spiration":

> Come quando una grossa nebbia spira,
>   o quando l'emisperio nostro annotta,
>   par di lungi un molin che'l vento gira. . .
> *Inferno* XXXIV, 4–7.

> As, when a thick mist blows, or when it is night in our hemisphere, a mill turned by the wind appears from afar.

Now, as for "spiration," when further on it is understood what the source of the cold wind which Dante had begun to feel over the ice of Cocito is, we know that if, as this simile suggests, that source were conceived as a windmill, it would be necessary to recognize that here functions are curiously reversed. This "mill" is not turned by the wind. It generates the wind by the movement of its wings. The verb "spirare" in fact is suggesting that this is a kind of "breathing forth."

Nothing short of a little excursion into the upper reaches of theology can serve to place us where we may see what is intended to be suggested here. And turning for this to St. Thomas Aquinas, we find the title of one of his articles on the Trinity to be *The Procession of the Divine Persons*.[19] Then under this heading we may read that there are in God two processions, that of the Word and Another:

> In evidence whereof we must observe that procession exists in God, only according to an action which does not tend to anything external, but remains in the agent itself. Such action in an intellectual

nature is that of the intellect and the will. The procession of the Word is by way of an intelligible operation ... besides the procession of the Word in God, there exists in Him another procession called the procession of Love.

And from a reply to an objection as part of this same article in the *Summa* our sense of possible relevance may be the further quickened:

... procession in God has no power or special name, except that of generation. Hence the procession which is not generation has remained without a special name; but it can be called *spiration*, as it is the procession of spirit.[20]

In subsequent articles we learn further that we may speak of four real relations in God: paternity, filiation, spiration and procession; that, as we have already been told, the processions are two only; that the procession of the Word covers the terms "paternity" and "filiation"; and, once more, that the procession of love has no proper name but is also called "spiration." All this is conveniently summed up when we come to the question dealing specifically with the "Person of the Holy Ghost":

... While there are two processions in God, one of these, the procession of love, has no proper name of its own, as stated above. Hence the relations also which follow from this procession are without a name: for which reason the Person proceeding in that manner has not a proper name. But as some names are accommodated by the usual mode of speaking to signify the aforesaid relations, as when we use the names of procession and spiration ... so to signify the divine Person, who proceeds by way of love, this name Holy Ghost [Spiritus Sanctus] is by use of scriptural speech accommodated to Him. .. For the name spirit in things corporeal seems to signify impulse and motion; for we call the breath and the wind by the term spirit. Now it is a property of love to move and impell the will of the lover towards the object beloved.[21]

In sum, the "procession" of the Holy Ghost is the procession of Love, for Love is the other name of the Third Person. Procession in this aspect is properly spiration: a breathing forth of love.

In so far as the triune Godhead is viewed in Its completely self-contained and eternal self-sufficiency, the Third Person is indeed understood to be that Love which the Father has for the Son and which the Son has for the Father. The tenth Canto of *Paradiso*, which presents to the wayfarer the souls of those who excelled in wisdom (and whose first spokesman is none other than Thomas Aquinas!), opens in this key:

> Guardando nel suo Figlio con l'Amore
> che l'uno e l'altro etternalmente spira,
> lo primo ed ineffabile Valore. . .
>
> *Paradiso* X, 1–4.

The first and ineffable Power, looking upon His Son with that Love which the one and the other eternally breathes forth. . .

But since it must needs be rather some spiration of love having relation with creatures outside of the agent which can more precisely meet the counterpart situation of Satan's condition, we do well to take in yet a further statement on this "spiration" in the *Summa:*

> . . . when the term love is taken in a notional sense it means nothing else than *to spirate love;* just as to speak is to produce a word, and to flower is to produce flowers. As therefore we say that a tree flowers by its flower, so do we say that the Father, by the Word, or the Son, speaks Himself and His creatures; and that the Father and the Son love each other *and us* by the Holy Ghost, or by Love proceeding.[22] [Italics mine.]

If three-headed Satan is the ironic counterpart of the triune God Whom he aspired to be, and if in theology, as we see, the notions of procession and spiration attach to the knowledge of the true Godhead, may not those same notions appear meaningful if seen to attach to the counterpart? They will indeed extend and enrich the meaning, the special sense of justice. And we can see now (and only now) that the color of the central face of Satan, being red, can very appropriately suggest (since red is most surely the color of love) that at the center of this triunity of Hell something which must be the opposite of love is to be seen and understood.[23] And as by way of the notion of spiration we bring into consideration, as an essential feature of the scene, that wind which moves out, "procedes," from Satan, we can indeed grasp that this hellish counterpart is actually spirating hate to his creatures—the opposite of love. Satan's relation to his "creatures" who dwell about him in the concentric circles of his "dolorous realm" is precisely the opposite of that of the true Emperor of the Empyrean. Thus the cold wind which forms the ice of Cocito is the ironic negation of that spiration of Love that moves the sun and all the stars, and whose warmth opens the rose of the blessed in the heaven of pure light.

If such an excursion in theology seems too lengthy a venture for what it brings to the poem, let it be remembered that this is a kind of knowledge which we must grant to Hugh's "spiritual" reader from the outset. Because he has it to begin with, and does not have to take time out to get it, the poet can call it up in him with the opening verse of a hymn, and with signs can introduce those notions of procession and spiration which extend so effectively the symbolism of a state of justice by which an archsinner ironically became so like what he aspired to be

A last note, touching not upon any particular symbolism as such, but upon that underlying sense of the transitive value of things in a created universe, which supports all medieval symbolism. Let the reader of the last canto of *Inferno* test this matter finally for himself. We come to Satan at the end of this long journey through Hell as to what we feel might easily have been conceived as a terminus, a fixed point at the center which is also the end: a kind of absolute pole of Evil counter-balancing that of the Supreme Good at the center and end of *Paradiso*. And in this sense a poet's eye could easily have rested upon Satan as upon such a goal. But what is most striking about the glance which takes in Satan at the last is its suggestion of just the opposite view. Nothing is terminal here. Indeed we do not even linger as long over the sight of the Emperor of this realm as we could have expected. Signs point beyond, even here. And Virgil soon is saying *tutto avem veduto* and is looking on to the climb out of Hell.

Evil has no positive or absolute existence. And a Christian poet's eye will not assign such value to it. Evil is only a negation of the one Absolute which is the Good.

Notes

1. Hebrews 11.

2. *Enarratio in Psalmum CXIII*, in *PL* 37, 1477: "Aegyptus autem, quoniam interpretatur Afflictio, vel Affligens, vel Comprimens, saepe imagine ponitur hujus saeculi."

3. Augustine, *Confessions*, I, 1.

4. Allen Tate, *On the Limits of Poetry* (New York, 1948), p. 113.

5. *De doctrina christiana*, I, 4.

6. *Eruditionis didascalicae liber septimus* in *PL*, vol. 176, 814.

7. Romans 1, 20; *cf.* II Corinthians 4, 18: "While we look not at the things which are seen, but at the things which are not seen: for the things which are seen are temporal; but the things which are not seen are eternal."

8. *Breviloquium*, pars II, 11., in *Opera omnia* (Quaracchi, 1882–1902).

9. For a fuller discussion of the metaphor of the "two books," see the author's *Essay on the Vita Nuova*, pp. 37 ff. and notes.

10. *Confessions*, X, 35.

11. In whose philosophy space itself becomes a contribution of the human mind.

12. *Summa theologica* II–II, 61, 4 *ad Resp.*: "Retaliation (*contrapassum*) denotes equal passion repaid for previous action; and the expression applied most properly to injurious persons and actions, whereby a man harms the person of his neighbor; for instance, if a man strike, that he be struck back. This kind of justice is laid down in the Law (Exodus 21, 23–24): He shall render life for life, eye for eye, etc."

13. See above, p. 25. Hugh has in mind, of course, St. Paul to the Corinthians (I, 2, 14–15): "But the natural man receiveth not the things of the spirit of God: for they are foolishness unto him; neither can he know them, because they are spiritually discerned. But he that is spiritual judgeth all things, yet he himself is judged of no man."

14. Isaiah 6, 2.

15. Isaiah 14, 14: "I will ascend above the heights of the clouds; I will be like the most high." St. Thomas Aquinas, *Summa theologica* I, 63, 3.

16. *Inferno* XXXIV, 28.

17. The full text of this hymn by Venantius Fortunatus will be found in F. Leo's edition of Fortunatus' *Opera poetica* (Berlin, 1881), p. 34. Versions in the modern Roman Breviary show some differences. On the hymn, the occasion of its composition and for further references, see John Julian, *A Dictionary of Hymnology* (London, 1951), p. 1220:
"Fortunatus was then living at Poictiers, where his friend, Queen Rhadegund, founded a nunnery. Before the consecration of the nunnery church she desired to present certain relics to it, and among these she obtained from the Emperor Justin II a fragment of the so-called True Cross, from which circumstance the nunnery received its name of the Holy Cross. This relic was sent in the first instance to Tours. . . In the Abbé E. Briand's *Sainte Radegunde* (Poitiers, 1887, pp. 128–30), its journey to Poictiers is thus described: 'Escorted by a numerous body of clergy and of the faithful holding lighted torches, the Bishop started in the midst of liturgical chants,

which ceased not to resound in honor of the hallowed wood of the Redemption. A league from Poictiers the pious cortege found the delegates of Rhadegund, Fortunatus at their head, rejoicing in the honor which had fallen to them; some carrying censers with perfumed incense, others torches of white wax. The meeting took place at Migné, at the place where twelve centuries and a half later, the cross appeared in the air. It was on this occasion [the coming of the cross to the nunnery] that the hymn *Vexilla Regis* was heard for the first time, the chant of triumph composed by Fortunatus to salute the arrival of the True Cross. . . It was the 19th of November, 569.' "

The hymn was thus primarily a processional hymn . . . one of the grandest hymns of the Latin church, in which he [the poet] in glowing accents invites us to contemplate the mystery of love accomplished on the Cross. The occasion thus gives the key to his choice of subject, and to most of the allusions throughout the hymn.

18. Fortunatus evidently had in mind, especially in stanza 5, the old legends of the Tree of the Cross, and designedly used in i., line 4, the word "patibulum" which means properly a cross, formed thus Y or thus Ⴤ , the latter form representing the stem of the tree, with the branches on which, as on a balance, the ransom of the world was weighed (stanza vi).

19. *Summa theologica*, I, Qu. 27.

20. Qu. 27, a. 4.

21. Qu. 36, a. 1, *ad Resp.*

22. Qu. 37, a. 2, *ad Resp.*

23. And once this point is certain, it follows that the colors of the other two faces will symbolize (as most commentators have seen) a *denial* of the other two Persons of the Trinity understood as Power and Wisdom; and will signify, accordingly, Impotence (black) and Ignorance (yellow).

24. On which fundamental point one might consult a very long tradition in Christian doctrine, of course, in which St. Augustine's writings against the Manicheans are basic: *PL*, 42 *passim* and especially col. 551.

The Pattern at the Center

The triumphal procession which comes in the forest at the top of the mountain of Purgatory is the triumph of Beatrice. This is known to us—or ought to be—once we have read the poem. But it is something we must *unknow* for purposes of reading the poem even a second time, if we are to find there, in the coming of Beatrice, that special kind of meaning which only an art form can give: a meaning emerging out of the unfolding of a particular form and from that process inseparable, indeed nonexistent. For, as the poem would have it, we come to Beatrice by a quite special way. And when we see her, finally, she stands framed in a meaning that is created and established by the very path of our approach. To point to this, of course, is to point to nothing new in poetry; but precisely to that kind of meaning with which students of literature as an art are first of all concerned—or ought to be.

The way to Beatrice in the poem is built along the line of a reader's expectation, an expectation which is planted in us by the words Virgil speaks to his charge in dismissing him at the edge of the garden:

Vedi lo sol che in fronte ti riluce;
  vedi l'erbetta, i fiori e li arbuscelli,
  che qui la terra sol da sé produce.
Mentre che vegnan lieti li occhi belli
  che, lacrimando, a te venir mi fenno,
  seder ti puoi e puoi andar tra elli.

Purgatorio XXVII, 133–138.

See the sun shining upon your face; see the grass, the flowers and the shrubs which here the earth produces by itself alone. While the beautiful eyes are coming in gladness which, in tears, caused me to come to you, you may sit among these things and you may go.

This can only be Beatrice who is expected. This is indeed only a reminder of what from the beginning we have known would come to pass when we reached this point in the journey.

As we move into the garden we come to a stream. Suddenly, in a meadow there beyond the stream, we see a maiden gathering flowers and singing as she goes. And we wonder: can this be Beatrice? No, it cannot be, for Dante does not appear to recognize her. This (we learn her name later) is Matelda. Dante may not yet cross the river and possess her, as he so much desires to do at once. But where is Beatrice? We were expecting her to come.

The stream along which we walked turns, so that in following it we face the east. Suddenly, throughout the forest there is a flash of light like lightning, and with it a sweet melody. And the poet breaks off his narrative to call upon all nine of the muses now for aid that he may set down in verses things hard to grasp in thought.

Is this Beatrice who is coming? Someone, surely, is coming; and coming as in some triumphal entry, for the melody, as it draws nearer, proves to be voices chanting and in the chant we make out the cry *Hosanna*.

Now with measured step a procession comes into view. It is one hard indeed to set down in prose, much less in verse, so is it laden with symbolic suggestion in all its detail. The poet, in the verses, brings it into view only gradually. We see the parts of it, one after another, in the strict order of their emerging. But, to get it before our mind's eye again, we may review this procession as it is displayed to our view *after* it has wholly emerged and come to a halt before us.

At the head of the whole, as it came forward, were seven lights or lamps, advancing as by miracle, since no bearers of these are visible. These lamps have left back over the whole procession seven bands or streamers of light which will continue to hang over it all the while, like a kind of heaven. Next, following the lamps, come twenty-four figures called elders (*seniori*), robed in white and distinct, as a first group in the procession, by virtue of the crowns of lilies which they wear. Next, following this first group and (as we come to see), at the center of the whole, come four strange wingèd animals, crowned in green. These, as they come, contain in the square of space between them another strange animal, half eagle and half lion, a gryphon, hitched to a two-wheeled chariot which it draws after it and at the wheels of which seven maidens are dancing. This central group is then followed by yet a third, made up of nine figures dressed in white like the first group of elders, but these with crowns of red.

This, of course, is to distinguish rapidly only the principal parts and more salient features of the procession as it halts there across the river. As we watched it (in the poem) come into view, a profusion of symbolic detail of color and gesture has helped us to see the parts for what they are and finally the whole for what it is. And we may safely assign names to the parts and to the whole.

The seven lights heading the procession and hanging back over it as a bright canopy are (in figure) the sevenfold gift of the Holy Spirit, the Spirit which presided over the writing of Holy Scripture and (for reasons we shall see) the same Spirit which the prophet Isaiah foretold would descend upon the Christ who was to come.[1] The procession, then, that follows the lights is unmistakably a procession of Holy Scripture itself. Here come now, not the authors of the books of Holy Scripture, but the books themselves and in the number and order in which they are (or were) known. First, all the books of the Old Testament, twenty-four of them, crowned in white, the color of faith. Next the four gospels, figured in the four strange animals, crowned in their turn in the color of hope. And last, as a third group, the remaining books of the New Testament crowned in the color of charity. In the figure bringing up the rear, we recognize Revelation.

But clearly more than the books of Scripture have a part in this procession. For at its center, contained by the four gospels, is a gryphon which, in its dual nature, figures Christ; and a chariot which is His Church. The seven maidens dancing at the wheels, four on one side and three on the other, are the moral and the theological virtues.

It is the chariot that marks the center of the whole procession. For one thing, when, at a signal like thunder, the whole comes to a halt, it is the chariot which is directly across the river from Dante—Dante who is and who remains our post of observation. Moreover, upon the halt of the whole parade, the elders who came ahead of the gryphon and His chariot, turn to face the chariot so that, in a quite literal sense, all eyes are upon the vehicle at the center.

But, now that we have the procession before us in its whole length and framed in this way, it is well to recall again that the poet does not give it to us so. On the contrary, he brings it into view in the manner of an emerging. We see successive parts only as these can be discerned from where Dante stands, gradually, one after the other, and in due order. The form here matters. For if this is Holy Scripture that comes here (and we know that it is), if this is the Word of God that comes so, we see that the poet has so managed the coming of that Word as to give us the distinct impression that it has unfolded before our eyes, that Scripture has come into view in the due order of its books, from the beginning to Revelation. By the form, by this process of unfolding, a dimension of meaning is put here that we must not miss. For, if this is the Word of God gradually emerging, where else could that take place if not in time? By such a form it is precisely *time* which is put here. And thereby is framed an aspect of symbolic significance which, I think, we may be helped to see by an observation on Holy Scripture which St. Bonaventura makes in the prologue to his *Breviloquium:*

Holy Scripture has a length which consists of the description of the times and ages, namely, from the beginning of the world to the day of judgment. . . Thus Scripture is of great length, because in its treatment it begins with the commencement of the world and of time, in the beginning of Genesis—and extends to the end of the world and of time, to the end of the Apocalypse.[2]

Bonaventura, we may be sure, was not the first to see in the length of Scripture this symbolic meaning. It is a meaning in symbol firmly enough established that a Christian poet can build with it.

It is at just the moment when the whole procession has fully emerged and halted before us that we can best feel the impact of the symbolic meaning. This, literally, is Holy Scripture coming in time. And now that it is all there before us, we have Scripture there as we, who come after its coming in time, do have it. This now is Scripture in that kind of timeless dimension in which it stands as it is spread in this life before the eyes of every faithful Christian. But St. Bonaventura has helped us to see more here, to see a figure of time itself unfolding from its beginning to its end. So now, how is it with time when the procession halts? Has time itself, in some way, come to a standstill? If so, then the pattern itself, in its symbolic dimension, is signifying something, is making a call which we should hear. It is signaling something. Must that not be this: that a day of Judgment is at hand?

Standing back thus and viewing the pattern of the whole, we do see that we have here, in figure, a conception of time, of history, that could not be more Christian.[3] First of all, time here has a beginning and an end. And, as time unfolds from its beginning to its end, there at the center is Christ and His Church. And now time is unfolded, time is come to a halt, time is immobilized, with all eyes on the center, and something, someone, expected there. In this most Christian pattern, will that not be one who comes to judge? And who could that be, if not Christ Himself? The very pattern of the procession before us seems now to be calling for Him to come.

In yet another way we can see that the scene before us is

making a most urgent call for something, for someone, to come there at the center. For the chariot there, we must not forget, is a triumphal chariot. Rome, the poem tells us, had no finer for its Caesar. It is a remarkable vehicle. And yet, surely, not the least remarkable thing about it is this: it is empty. There is no one in triumph on this triumphal chariot; and since there is no one there, surely someone is expected there. The elders have turned and faced it. All eyes that came before it and all that came after it are now upon it. Is Christ to appear upon it? But is not Christ given here in the procession by the gryphon who pulls the chariot? And were we not expecting Beatrice?

We go back thus to that expectation as to a thread that can guide us through all this by revealing to us, as we move along it, the certain outline of a poet's intention. We expect Beatrice. But all the while everything, the pattern of the whole, the image of time immobilized and expectant at its center, all seems to call for Christ.

It is indeed time to go back and remember that this thread of an intention becomes especially clear as the procession unfolds, for as it advances we hear utterances, cries and shouts that are an unmistakable part of that intention. First, as the chanting came nearer, it was the cry *Hosanna* that we heard. Then, as they came forward with their eyes upon the guiding spirit of the Lord, the books of the Old Testament—those forward-looking and prophetic books—shouted in unison what is surely the salutation of Gabriel to Mary: "Benedicta tue nelle figlie d'Adamo."

Can those words be heralding anything if not the Christ who is to come? But as we came into this garden, we had been given to expect Beatrice. Indeed, when the procession halts and those elders have turned about to face the empty chariot, one of them (unmistakably the Song of Solomon) utters another welcoming cry which would seem to call now for some lady to come. Thrice he shouts "Veni sponsa de Libano" and clearly the spectator (and reader) is expected to hear the word which follows upon that utterance in the Canticle itself and completes it: *Coronaberis* ("thou shalt be crowned").

Tota pulchra es, amica mea,
et macula non est in te.
Veni de Libano, sponsa mea,
veni de Libano, veni, *coronaberis.*[4]

Then finally, when all is halted, and when all eyes are upon the empty chariot, we see appear upon it, first, many angels who arise with a welcoming cry, calling in their turn now for the one who is to come. And their shout is: *Benedictus qui venis.* The poet could have had it "Benedicta quae venis" without the slightest metrical difficulty. But no, the cry is Benedic*tus.* Surely a poet could not more clearly reveal his guiding intention.

Moreover the very image by which Beatrice does, at long last, come to stand upon the chariot is the final seal upon this intention. For the figure by which she appears is that of the sun rising behind morning mists. We may note first of all, of course, the accuracy of the image with respect to the immediate situation. We remember that we are still facing the east, that it is early morning in the garden. Then, on the chariot, there arise figures, tossing flowers so as to make a veritable cloud of these. And within, or rather through, that cloud Beatrice appears. The image is accurate. But it is designed to be more than that, to fulfill a larger purpose and pattern, and this we are now in a better position to see. For we must know that the image of a rising sun could bring with it, out of a long traditional usage, an established burden of symbolic meaning. A rising sun was the image for Christ, the established image for the coming of Christ.[5] Later, in Paradise, we may even see the confirmation of this. For there, where Christ comes in what is truly His triumph, He comes as a sun.[6] And here now, at the center, where the very configuration of the procession itself has seemed to call for Him, here now, as angels strew a cloud of flowers in the air and shout *Benedictus qui venis,* here Beatrice is at last given to us by the very image which, for so long before, had given Christ in His coming:

Io vidi già nel cominciar del giorno
la parte oriental tutta rosata,
e l'altro ciel di bel sereno adorno;
e la faccia del sol nascere ombrata,

sì che, per temperanza di vapori,
l'occhio la sostenea lunga fiata:
così dentro una nuvola di fiori
  che da le mani angeliche saliva
  e ricadeva in giù dentro e di fori,
sovra candido vel cinta d'uliva
  donna m'apparve. . .

Purgatorio XXX, 22–23.

At times I have seen, at the start of day, the east all rosy and
the rest of the sky adorned with beautiful serenity; and the
face of the sun rise overcast, so that, through its being tempered
by mists, the eye could endure it a long while.

So, within a cloud of flowers rising from angels' hands and
falling again within and without, crowned with olive over a
white veil, dressed in the color of living flame beneath a cloak
of green, a lady appeared to me. . .

At last there is someone in triumph upon the chariot at the
center. What in so many ways was called for is now delivered.
A pattern is fulfilled. It is not Christ who comes. It is Beatrice—
Beatrice who comes *as* Christ.

But we have yet to observe here an even more striking point
of detail. The pattern before us, as we saw, was not signaling
merely *a* coming of Christ. But, because the procession of
Scripture could symbolize time itself; and, as it came to a halt,
could suggest time at an end; because we could feel that now
we had before us somehow time at a standstill, with all eyes on
the center, we could sense the signal (this being the Christian
pattern of time that it is) that a day of Judgment might be at
hand.

Is this particular of the pattern fulfilled? Is this signal of a
day of Judgment met and answered when Beatrice does come?
Yes, even this. We get, in a simile, the first confirmation of it.
For, as the angels rise up on the chariot, scattering their cloud
of flowers and shouting their cry of welcome (*Benedictus qui
venis*), the manner of their rising there is said to be as that of
the saints shall be on the day of the Resurrection:

Quali i beati al novissimo bando
  surgeran presti ognun di sua caverna,
  la revestita voce alleluiando;
cotali in su la divina basterna

si levar cento, ad vocem tanti senis,
   ministri e messaggier di vita etterna.
Tutti dicean: *"Benedictus qui venis!"*
                                    Purgatorio XXX, 12–19.

As the blessed at the last Trump will rise ready each from his tomb, singing Hallelujah with reclad voice, so upon the divine chariot, *ad vocem tanti senis,* rose up a hundred ministers and messengers of life eternal, who all cried, *"Benedictus qui venis!"*

It is a figure almost too transparent in the way it reveals a poet's intention. There may be no mistake about it. The coming of Beatrice has completely fulfilled the demands of the pattern. As Christ will come at His second coming, so does Beatrice come here: in a cloud of glory, at the end of time and at the center of time—to judge. The analogue is complete.

*   *   *

For we soon see that Beatrice has come to judge, to stand in sternest judgment on one whose name is the first word she utters: Dante.

And we hear from her now the reproaches by which we are reminded of the role she had had in the poet's life. Beatrice goes over the facts of the past, reads them out of the Book of Memory. (*Thou art worthy to take the book and open the seals thereof.*)[7] The *Comedy* here gathers into itself the experience of the *Vita Nuova,* may be said to build on to the earlier work. Among her reproaches we have, in a single terzina, the statement of the part she had played in Dante's life in her brief time on earth:

Alcun tempo il sostenni col mio volto:
   mostrando li occhi giovanetti a lui,
   meco il menava in dritta parte volto.
                                    Purgatorio XXX, 121–123.

For a time I sustained him with my face: letting him see my young eyes, I guided him turned in the right direction.

By such a role she had deserved the name *salute* so often assigned to her in the *Vita Nuova;* indeed, had so earned her own true name, *Beatrice.* She had died. And now, ten years later, she comes from above and beyond to judge him, comes with a charge of the backsliding of which he is guilty in the years since her death:

> Quando di carne a spirto era salita,
>   e bellezza e virtù cresciuta m'era,
>   fu'io a lui men cara e men gradita;
> e volse i passi suoi per via non vera,
>   imagini di ben seguendo false,
>   che nulla promission rendono intera.
> Nè l'impetrare ispirazion mi valse,
>   con le quali ed in sogno e altrimenti
>   lo rivocai; sì poco a lui ne calse!
> Tanto giù cadde, che tutti argomenti
>   a la salute sua eran già corti,
>   fuor che mostrarli le perdute genti.
> Per questo visitai l'uscio de'morti,
>   e a colui che l'ha qua su condotto,
>   li preghi miei, piangendo, furon porti.
>
> *Purgatorio* XXX, 127–141.

When I had arisen from flesh to spirit, and my beauty and virtue had increased, I was less dear to him and less cherished; and he turned his steps along an untrue way, following after false images of good which yield no promise to the full. Nor did obtaining inspirations avail me, with which both in dreams and otherwise I called him back: so little did he care about it! He fell so low that all measures for his salvation were by then insufficient except by showing him the lost people. Therefore I visited the gate of the dead, and, with tears, to him who has lead him up here, my entreaties were taken.

Let this be observed first of all: the analogy of Beatrice to Christ, built up before our eyes in the last cantos of the *Purgatorio*, is no arbitrary, no ornamental, way devised by a poet to praise his lady. It is in Beatrice's role in Dante's life that that analogy finds its full and impressive support. We must hold the *Vita Nuova* and the *Comedy* together at this point (and this is something which the *Comedy* here invites us to do) if we are to see this. We know from the *Vita Nuova* how Beatrice had come into the poet's life as a miracle, as a love descending from Heaven to light an upward way to salvation.[8] And now we learn from her reproaches that, after her death, she had come again to him in visions to recall him to the supernal goal. We have

known, too, from the beginning of the poem, what she recounts
here: that for him she had descended to Hell, to Virgil in Limbo,
to lay open the way to salvation. Analogy is not an equivalence.
Analogy is a resemblance. Clearly these things do reflect other
things: the coming of Another Love upon earth, the descent of
Another to Hell, the coming of Another in visions after His
death. But, now that we are holding the *Vita Nuova* and the
Comedy together and reading the story which they together
tell, I would point out one aspect of the whole analogy which
seems till now to have escaped our notice—a most central aspect.
An attentive reader of the *Vita Nuova* of course knows that the
earlier work itself pointed up an analogy Beatrice–Christ–did
so, indeed so boldly that a later century, the sixteenth, unable to
understand that this was analogy, expurgated the work in its
first printed edition, deleting the closing words of Chapter XXIV,
for instance, where we read how the poet one day had seen
Beatrice coming in the company of another gentle lady and
following after this lady as she came:

> . . . io vidi venire verso me una gentile donna, la quale era di famosa
> bieltade, e fue già molto donna di questo primo mio amico. E lo
> nome di questa donna era Giovanna, salvo che per la sua bieltade,
> secondo che altri crede, imposto l'era nome Primavera; e così era
> chiamata. E appresso lei, guardando, vidi venire la mirabile Beatrice.
> Queste donne andaro presso di me così l'una appresso l'altra, e parve
> che Amore mi parlasse nel cuore, e dicesse: "Quella prima è nom-
> inata Primavera solo per questa venuta d'oggi; chè io mossi lo im-
> ponitore del nome a chiamarla così Primavera, cioè prima verrà lo
> die che Beatrice si mosterrà dopo la imaginazione del suo fedele. E
> se anche vogli considerare lo primo nome suo, tanto è quanto dire
> 'prima verrà', però che lo suo nome Giovanna è da quello Giovanni
> lo quale precedette la verace luce, dicendo: 'Ego vox clamantis in
> deserto: parate viam Domini'."
>
> *Vita Nuova*, Chapter XXIV.

I saw coming toward me a gentle lady who was famous for her
beauty and who had formerly been very much the lady of this first
friend of mine. And the name of this lady was Joan except that because of her beauty, as some believe, she had been given the name
Primavera; and so was she called. These ladies passed near me thus
one after the other, and it seemed to me that Love spoke to me in my
heart and said: "She who comes first is named Primavera for just
this her coming today; because I moved the giver of the name to

name her thus *Primavera*, that is, *prima verrà* on that day when
Beatrice will appear after the imagination of her faithful one. And
if you will also consider her first name, it is tantamount to saying
'prima verrà' because her name Joan is from that John who preceded
the True Light saying: *Ego vox clamantis in deserto; parate viam
Domini.*"

Certainly the poet has not wanted us to miss this analogy—
one indeed already manifest in the chapter immediately preceding
this, the twenty-third (which could thus hardly be nearer the
center of the *Vita Nuova*) a chapter where, in a vision which came
to him as he lay sick of a fever, the death of Beatrice is an-
nounced to the poet amid signs of universal cataclysm that can
only remind us of the death of Christ (and, by yet other signs,
of His Ascension):

Così cominciando ad errare la mia fantasia, venni a quello ch'io non
sapea ove io mi fosse; e vedere mi parea donne andare scapigliate
piangendo per via, maravigliosamente triste; e pareami vedere lo sole
oscurare, sì che le stelle si mostravano di colore ch'elle mi faceano
giudicare che piangessero; e pareami che li uccelli volando per l'aria
cadessero morti, e che fossero grandissimi terremuoti. E maraviglian-
domi in cotale fantasia, e paventando assai, imaginai alcuno amico
che mi venisse a dire: "Or non sai? la tua mirabile donna è partita di
questo secolo." Allora cominciai a piangere molto pietosamente; e
non solamente piangea ne la imaginazione, ma piangea con li occhi,
bagnandoli di vere lagrime. Io imaginava di guardare verso lo cielo, e
pareami vedere moltitudine d'angeli li quali tornassero in suso, ed
aveano dinanzi da loro una nebuletta bianchissima. A me parea che
questi angeli cantassero gloriosamente, e le parole del loro canto mi
parea udire che fossero queste: *Osanna in excelsis. . .*

Vita Nuova, Chapter XXIII.

Thus, as my phantasy began to wander, I came to such a point that
I did not know where I was: and I seemed to see women going along
a way, weeping and disheveled, marvelously sad: and I seemed to see
the sun grow dark so that the stars came out with a color that made
me judge them to be weeping; and it seemed to me that the birds
flying through the air fell and that there were very great earth-
quakes. And marveling in such a phantasy and being greatly afraid, I
imagined that some friend came to me and said: "But don't you
know? Your marvelous lady is gone from this world." Then I began
to weep most piteously; . . . I imagined that I looked toward Heaven
and I seemed to see a host of angels that were returning upwards

and they had before them a very white little cloud. It seemed to me that these angels sang gloriously and the words of their song, I seemed to hear, were these: *Hosanna in excelsis. . .*

Why we have not seen it before, I do not know. Here are the reproaches of Beatrice inviting us to hold the *Vita Nuova* and the *Divine Comedy* together. Now do we not see what may be seen only if we do this? In the *Vita Nuova*, at the center of *Vita Nuova*, Beatrice is seen to depart this life, uplifted in the company of a host of angels, in a cloud, and the cry that accompanies her is *Hosanna*. At the center of the *Divine Comedy*, Beatrice comes, Beatrice returns, in the company of a host of angels, in a cloud of glory, and in a company whose first cry is again *Hosanna*. But what is more striking than all of these details is this: Beatrice's death at the center of the *Vita Nuova* is like Christ's death. We have seen the signs—like Christ's death and like an ascension. And at the center of the *Comedy*, Beatrice's return, what is thus literally Beatrice's second coming, resembles not *a* coming of Christ, but the *second* coming of Christ—in a day of Judgment.

The *Comedy* is built on to the *Vita Nuova* more essentially than we have imagined; we have only to look at the pattern which the one work and the other bears at its center.

We have been speaking of the last cantos of the *Purgatorio* as the center of the *Comedy*. But in what sense is this so? Is not the middle of the *Purgatorio* the center—cantos 16, 17, 18, where the great questions of love and free will are discussed? Yes, if we count the cantos. But if we will look, not at the surface symmetry of the poem, but somewhat deeper; if we will but consider the whole as an action, we shall see that at either end of that action, we are outside of time. Hell is beyond time, an eternal place. So too, of course, is the last heaven of light where God is. But from the first canto of *Purgatory* up to the Empyrean, in that area, that is, of the action that lies between these two eternal poles and timeless termini, we are in time, we move in time. Just so much of this upward way to God is through time. And now we see that when Beatrice comes, she comes at the center of this stretch in time. It is as if the procession at the center, in so far as that could suggest in its unfolding the whole extent of time, had also held out the symbol of this. For, there, in a stretch of time so signified, Beatrice comes at the center. And so too in the upward action of the poem. Let there be a vertical line, a line of ascent in time in the upward way to God. And let there be a horizontal line, as it were, drawn across this vertical line by a procession symbolizing time. Where these lines meet, where these lines cross in the poem—there Beatrice comes—as Christ.[9]

Holding before us now what has been observed and standing back somewhat from the *Comedy*, we must see in this pattern at the center of the larger work certainly more than simply the continuation of an analogy Beatrice–Christ already built into the structure of the *Vita Nuova*. I would not exclaim here over another little symmetry of pattern or another rare correspondence of detail in Dante's work. We have to do here with something as profoundly essential as it is central.

What this is I may only briefly suggest. Clearly, we have here yet another manifestation of what we already had had glimpses of as the guiding principle of construction for this most Christian of poets. Before now we have recognized that with his triple rhyme Dante built everywhere into the structure of his creation a sign which the created universe itself everywhere displayed: the marks, the vestiges, left by a triune Architect. The poem, in fine, declares everywhere, with its terza rima, that it is an analogue to God's "poem," to God's book of the created universe. And even as all things in that universe reveal among themselves an order, so the parts of Dante's poem in its symmetries. Before now, too, we have recognized that the poet's style and his allegory both find their unique model in God's other book, in Holy Scripture. So that the poem is, in yet other significant respects, an analogue of God's way of building, and of God's way of writing. Before now, in short, we have known that this poet's work displayed analogy to God's work. And now shall we not see, in the pattern here discerned at the very center of the whole, the most striking manifestation yet of Dante's "imitation," and of the implicit canon of art by which a Christian poet did his work? For at the center of time and history, as God built time and history in His "poem," Christ comes and dies—and then will come again. So at the center of this Christian poet's work, we catch twice the reflection of the great model by which he built: at the center of the *Vita Nuova*, Beatrice's death like Christ's and her departure like an ascension; and at the center of the *Divine Comedy* Beatrice coming in what is her second coming as Christ will come in His. A human poem is thus by analogy participating in a divine poem, can be seen to be made in its image. In so doing, a poem does what all created things do in a Christian universe, a poem participates in true existence, in Being.[10] We shall be better readers of this poet's work when we shall have learned to follow out the unfolding of its form as the fulfillment of a necessary pattern; a pattern by which a Christian poem has its meaning—which, for this poem, at least, is that intelligibility by which it ultimately has its being.

Notes

1. Isaiah 11, 2: "Et requiescet super eum spiritus Domini: spiritus sapientiae et intellectus, spiritus consilii et fortitudinis, spiritus scientiae et pietatis; et replebit eum spiritus timoris Domini." *Cf. Convivio* IV, xxi, 11 ff.

The point of importance is that, by way of the prophetic nature of the passage in Isaiah and its vision *of the Christ to come*, we have in this feature of the procession (and at the very beginning) the kind of signal which can coöperate with the others in this respect.

2. *Opera omnia* (Quaracchi, 1891) Tome V, p. 203: "De longitudine sacrae Scripturae." *See also* at the end of this chapter: "Et quia nullus homo tam longaevus est quod totam possit videre oculis carnis suae, nec futura potest per se praevidere; providit nobis Spiritus Sanctus librum Scripturae sacrae, cuius longitudo commetitur se decursui regiminis universi."

3. On the essential features of such a Christian conception of history a number of important studies may be consulted: O. Cullman, *Christ and Time*, trans. Filson (Philadelphia, 1950); R. Niebuhr, *Faith and History* (New York, 1949); E. C. Rust, *The Christian Understanding of History* (London, 1947); P. Tillich, *The Interpretation of History*, trans. Rasetzki and Talmey (New York, 1936); and the important article by J. Daniélou, "The Problem of Symbolism," in *Thought* XXV (1950), 423 ff. Also the brief but most illuminating essay by E. Frank, "St. Augustine and Greek Thought" (Cambridge, Mass., The Augustinian Society, 1942), p. 11: "The Epiphany of Christ was the center of his [Augustine's] historical speculation."

4. Canticum Canticorum 4, 8. The King James Version does not translate the "coronaberis," so important for our considerations.

5. On the Sun image in this respect, *see* especially H. F. Dunbar, *Symbolism in Medieval Thought*, etc. (New Haven, 1929), pp. 105 ff. and *passim*.

6. *Paradiso* XXIII, 29.

7. Revelation 5, 8–9: "And when he had taken the book, the four beasts and the four and twenty elders fell down before the Lamb . . . and they sung a new song, saying, Thou art worthy . . ., etc."

8. For a full discussion of this aspect of the *Vita Nuova see* the author's *Essay on the Vita Nuova* especially Chapter III, "From Love to Caritas." *See also* for the analogy Beatrice-Christ and the pattern at the center in that work.

9. *Cf.* P. Tillich, *The Protestant Era*, trans. Adams (Chicago, 1948), p. 19: "This became obvious in the last creation of original Greek thought, Neo-Platonism, in which the horizontal line is entirely negated by the vertical one, and society is entirely devaluated for the sake of the individual soul. The emanation of the different degrees of reality from the ultimate One to mere matter and the return of the soul through the different spheres from matter to the ultimate One stabilize a vertical direction of thinking and acting which has nothing to do with the horizontal line and the directed time of history." However this may be in fact, it seems clear that Dante has staged, in symbol, the crossing of these two lines.

10. On the doctrine of analogy and of participation in being, consult E. Gilson, *The Spirit of Mediaeval Philosophy*, trans. Downes (New York, 1936), chapter on "Analogy, Causality and Finality" and *passim*.

The Substance of Things Seen

"As a thing is related to existence, so is it related to truth," wrote Dante to Can Grande, quoting Aristotle.[1] He was presenting only a part of his poem to the Lord of Verona, and yet, to explain the part, he had first to introduce the whole. And he meant these words from the *Metaphysics* to apply to the whole *Commedia*. That they do apply, we have abundantly seen in distinguishing three dimensions of the poem's structure: its allegory, its symbolism and the pattern of analogy which it displays so impressively at its center. It is, however, the dimension of analogy in the broadest sense which can be seen to be the comprehensive principle by which the poem is related to existence and exhibits truth. Both the other two aspects, the allegory and the symbolism, can be seen to fall within the category of analogy: the allegory being so constructed as to be in the image of God's allegory in His book of Scripture, where events themselves are seen to point beyond to other events; and its symbolism so devised as to be made in the image of the real world of God's creation, God's other book, wherein things are also signs. Then, at its center, the poem reveals its analogy to the structure of history; and history, too, is God's work. Thus, on a general principle of analogy, the poem is related to an existence which could not be more fundamentally Christian and which, therefore, Aristotle could hardly have dreamt of in his philosophy. This relation, in Dante's view, would be the poem's truth. The Christian poet has "imitated" the best possible model, the truest existence known to him. His fiction, by the principle affirmed, could not be "truer."

It is important to see this, for if we lose sight of it we run the risk of losing sight of the poem. The poem is distinguishable from Scripture and from reality and from history in its being a fiction. Its distance from its three models (and, that is, the distance from existence) is the very condition by which it can be true. In the Christian view, both the distance and the relation would seem to be that which any created thing must bear to existence. Yet this created thing is man's work, not God's. The relation is therefore not quite so simple.

Let it be observed at this point that nothing within this poem ever declares that it is a fiction. The fiction of the *Divine Comedy* is that it is not fiction. And no work ever guarded that fundamental hypothesis more carefully. Nowhere in the work is this vision of things beyond presented as a vision[2] or a dream. These things happened, and the poet who went that way in the flesh and experienced them is, now that he has returned, a scribe who sets them down as they had occurred. The Muses, to be sure, are invoked, the scribe is also the poet aware of the inspiration which comes from them and from above, and of the need of it. But that inspiration served only to enable him to set down in verse what had once been in fact. We think of Milton. Neither is his action given as a fiction. Yet *Paradise Lost* is a vision.

But if, on the face of it, it seems natural enough that a fiction should protect itself from any undermining awareness of illusion, we may think of what a Renaissance poet two centuries later does in this regard. Ariosto's romance deals, in its basic fiction, with what are, after all, presented as historical events. History reports these deeds of Charlemagne and his paladins in their struggle against the invading Saracens. It is the postulate of his poem too, therefore, that these *gesta* are not invented. And yet, as every reader of the *Orlando Furioso* knows, within the cantos and particularly at the beginning of cantos, one meets that voice of the poet speaking out to declare, within the work and with his peculiar irony, that these deeds are invented, that they are spun out of a poet's brain, that it is he who weaves. The poet, as he steps thus onto the stage, smiles at his fabric—and we find ourselves smiling with him.

The *Furioso*, we may pause to reflect, does not display an analogical relation to existence (at least as Dante and the medieval view conceived existence). That very number three which everywhere was seen to shine through existence is made the basic unit of structure in the *Comedy*, causing it to hang together like a chain suspended from its triune End. But Ariosto's stanza of eight verses is a discreet little unit of narration in itself, sealing itself off each time with a closing couplet at the end. Such a unit could often be dropped out of the sequence without its loss being noticed at all. Or we may think, beyond the mere verse form, of the spirit of Ariosto's most acentric world and then of what we have seen at the center of Dante's poem. The distance could not be greater.

Within the fiction of Dante's *Comedy* the basic postulate is always protected. But should it happen that this structure really ceased to be viewed by us as a fiction, then the poem could no longer be a poem, it would merge with the existence lying around it and we should lose what is most precious to us: a form which detaches itself from ambient existence by mirroring it, by staging before the mind in form objectified its relation to that existence.

There is a point in his *Soliloquies* where St. Augustine seems to have focused upon this matter of the possible truth of "things staged" and to have found it a "marvelous thing"; and since his conception of truth lies so near to Dante's, in spite of their distance in time, it seems worth while to attend to what he says there. The dialogue has at this point turned to consider the "works of men" and the truth which these can give. "Reason" is speaking to Augustine:

Thus these works of men themselves, such as comedies or tragedies, or mimes, and other such things, we may class with the works of painters and sculptors. For a painted man cannot be so true, however he may tend into the form of man, as those things which are written in the books of the comic poets. For neither do they will to be false, nor are they false by any desire of their own; but by a certain necessity, so far as they have been able to follow the intention of the author. But on the stage Roscius in will was a false Hecuba, in nature a true man; but by that will also a true tragedian, in that he was fulfilling the thing proposed: but a false Priam, in that he made himself like Priam, but was not he. From which now arises a certain marvelous thing, which nevertheless no one doubts to be so. *Augustine:* What, pray, is it? *Reason:* What think you, unless that all these things are in certain aspects true, by this very thing that they are in certain aspects false, and that for their quality of truth this alone avails them, that they are false in another regard? Whence to that which they either will or ought to be, they in no wise attain, if they avoid being false. For how could he whom I have mentioned [Roscius] have been a true tragedian, had he been unwilling to be a false Hector, a false Andromache, a false Hercules, and innumerable other things? or how would a picture, for instance, be a true picture, unless it were a false horse? or how could there be in a mirror a true image of man, if it were not a false man? Wherefore, if it avails some things that they be somewhat false in order that they may be somewhat true; why do we so greatly dread falsity, and seek truth as the greatest good?[*]

If we but direct Reason's view of this "marvelous" consideration to Dante's "comedy" and to the question of its relation to existence, we find it most illuminating and pertinent, arising as it does within a Christian frame of mind. We grasp how it avails some things to be false—we may read "fictive"—in order that they may be true. And we find ourselves standing back from the *Comedy* and eyeing it, in such a focus, as myth. But what kind of myth is it?

We may hardly let our thought move along this line without thinking of Plato and of his concern with the truth of myth. Now we know that with Plato it is possible to turn from the mythmaker to the philosopher and to ask the latter why he indulged in myth at all.[4] Mythmaker and philosopher are the same person and because they are, the question makes sense. But with Dante it does not make at least the same sense. Dante is no philosopher and quite readily admitted as much. And while in his critical works there are passages which give us his way of reflecting on poetry and on his own poetry (which he does not ever call myth), these do not constitute a philosophy. And yet Dante had a philosophy. We quite properly call him a philosophical poet. Only, of course, it is not his philosophy as Plato's is Plato's. With Dante the philosophy is also a faith; is first of all a faith, well buttressed with authority and one shared by most of the Western world of his time.

If for a moment we try to see through Plato's eyes, we are bound to see Dante's philosophy as no philosophy at all. And if we turn to a philosopher of Dante's time, to Thomas Aquinas for instance, we do not find in him at all the thinker after Plato's heart. Neither Socrates nor Plato would have understood what Thomas was about; nor could they have seen his *Summa* as anything but a curious attempt to explore the rational content of a myth. The Socratic dialectic keeps to a human position. It has its being in a group of men where the speaker pauses now and again to say: "Do you agree? If you agree, then I may proceed." That kind of reasoning was no more predominant in Dante's time. The first and last authority is no longer in man but outside of man. The human position as ultimate umpire is, in a sense, gone. It is now no question (or at least not first of all a question) of agreement between one man and another. The agreement is to be between man and a body of writing which is taken to be the truth divinely revealed to man; and only if Holy Scripture, not man, agrees with what is said, may the argument proceed. Man and all man's powers of intellect are rounded with a faith outside of which there is no truth that matters. Plato sits in the first circle of Dante's Hell with Aristotle because he, like the *maestro di color che sanno*, failed to believe what they could only have considered to be a myth: namely, that the time would come when the word of God would be made flesh and dwell among us. To Augustine Plato was very nearly "divine." But there was one truth (and it the only truth that really mattered) which Augustine did not find in the Platonists: "But that the Word was made flesh and dwelt among us I did not find there." [5]

It cannot be our purpose to expound here the general agreement or disagreement between Platonism and Christianity. However, the ultimate implications of the disagreement may not be ignored; for the disagreement means that from Plato's vantage point within free reason both Aquinas and Dante, both the Christian philosopher and the Christian poet, are working within a myth. Thomas (with considerable help from Aristotle) is seeing how far reason can go in company with it. And we are trying to say what Dante is doing.

Thomas knew that reason did not go all the way; that it did not, in fact, go very far. The Revelation of the truth had come too great a distance in order to reach us. Here, from the *Summa contra gentiles*, in brief is Thomas' statement of his epistemology regarding things divine:

> Man has three kinds of knowledge of divine things. The first of these is according as man, by the natural light of reason, ascends through creatures into the knowledge of God; the second is in so far as the divine truth, exceeding human understanding, descends to us by way of revelation, not however as though demonstrated to our sight, but as set forth in words to be believed; the third is according as the human mind is elevated to the perfect intuition of the things that are revealed.[6]

These are three ways to knowledge which one needs to remember in reading Dante's *Commedia*. As for the province claimed here for natural reason, it is evident that the famous formula *fides quaerens intellectum* still fits even it. It should occur to us in fact that positions here compared with those in Plato's philosophy are strangely reversed. For if you will allow the *fides* to be undogmatic, something which can spring eternal in the human heart, then faith seeking understanding fits Plato the mythmaker and not the philosopher. It is, for instance, a formula which says very well what Socrates is doing in his last moments in myth before drinking the poison. Plato the philosopher could smile down on the myth from a superior position in free reason and could say that such talk as this was needed only because there was a part of man that required it. Without the myth the argument would be incomplete because without it the whole man would not be satisfied. We are able to turn to the philosopher Plato and to get that answer to the question: "Why the myth?" Instead, finding Christian philosophy within the myth, we cannot ask it that question. We are obliged to ask the

Christian philosopher not "why the myth?" but rather "why the reason?" And then, *mutatis mutandis*, the Christian answer is not unlike Plato's. Faith now smiles down on reason and observes that in the end we need reason and indulge in it only because without it there would be a part of man unsatisfied. There is in man this natural desire to know. And it is not bad, it is indeed right, that the whole man should be satisfied. Now, with more reason than ever, we may ask, where is the need for Dante's way of seeing? Who calls for the mythmaker within the myth? Not Thomas Aquinas. Faith alone can give all that is needed for salvation, only to faith Thomas, because of the whole man, has added reason. But who asks to see as Dante sees? Not the theologian, not the philosopher of Dante's day, not the mystic who rather than seeing seeks to lose himself in direct and momentary union with God. Then why see as Dante saw? It may take some time to answer that question and if in the end we may seem to have found the suggestion of an answer, it will be for the most part on speculative grounds. A reply can be had from Dante's work up to a point. Beyond that we are guessing. Beyond that we are indulging in myth.

In Chapter XXV of the *Vita Nuova* Dante breaks off his narrative in order to step out upon the stage as author and state his attitude toward a certain myth.[7] Up to that point in both the poems and the prose, Love has been presented as the God of Love of troubadour renown and therefore as a person. He has come as such a god in a first vision bearing Beatrice in his arms; later he has appeared as a pilgrim giving advice to Dante in the conduct of his love; and then he has been seen as a young man dressed in white sitting beside the poet's bed, weeping—all this before Chapter XXV. But now the author seems eager to square this matter with the truth. And Love, he says, to tell the truth, is not a person. The opening words of this chapter are these:

Potrebbe qui dubitare persona degna da dichiararle onne dubitazione, e dubitare potrebbe di ciò, che io dico d'Amore come se fosse una cosa per sè, e non solamente sustanzia intelligente, ma sì come fosse sustanzia corporale: la quale cosa, secondo la veritate, è falsa; chè Amore non è per sè sì come sustanzia, ma è uno accidente in sustanzia.

> Some person worthy of having his doubts made clear might here question that I write of Love as if it were a thing *per se*, and not only an intelligent substance but even as if it were a corporeal substance: which, according to the truth, is false; for Love is not a thing *per se* as a substance is, but is an accident in a substance.

The terminology is scholastic. Love, in other words, is no person. Love is a quality occurring in persons. And having declared what is the truth, Dante goes on to justify this seeming departure from it, this license of personification. He finds it very common among the ancient poets and argues that modern poets have every right to do what ancient poets did. We smile. But it may be that we smile before we understand what Dante is about. In the first place, the argument gives Dante a chance to lay down a law for modern poets. When the ancient poets used personification, he says, they knew what they were doing. They did not do this without reason, but with reason. Nor must modern poets do so without reason. For it would be a great shame, says Dante, were a poet asked to give an account in prose (that is, according to reason) of what he had said in a poem (that is, according to imagination), and were unable to do so.

This can easily appear to be a statement of a doctrine of allegory. It has in fact been taken as such. C. S. Lewis, for instance, in his study *The Allegory of Love*, has pointed to it as that passage in which Dante speaks as the master of allegory that he was.[8] But I beg to differ with Mr. Lewis and with yet better *dantisti* than he lays claim to be. The *Vita Nuova* is no allegory. The work is full of symbolism and mystical analogy, but symbol and analogy are not allegory. The *Roman de la Rose* is an allegory. The rose has another meaning and there is a key for it. But in the *Vita Nuova* there is nothing of this. What does Beatrice mean besides Beatrice or the protagonist Dante besides just himself? Until Lewis or somebody has answered that question and in ways that are not simply quite impossible to follow out in the reading of the work, we shall continue to read the *Vita Nuova* without finding allegory in it. For not even Love stood for something else. You cannot now turn back from Chapter XXV and wherever Love appears, read "an accident in a substance." This chapter proclaims, not allegory, but the responsibility of poets to truth. Poets must always be able if asked, to give an account, according to the truth, of what they have said. If they have talked about Love, they must know what Love is. That is all. Plato spoke of two kinds of lies: the true lie and the untrue lie. Only the poet who knows the truth can tell the true lie.[9] And Dante is here insisting that poets should know the truth.

It is a point in the *Vita Nuova* which Plato would have applauded: that point where Dante begins to distinguish the true lie from the untrue. Not in definition alone; there is artistic strategy here as well. For as one reads on past Chapter XXV, it becomes clear that in defining Love according to the truth, Dante has done something more. Love as a person does not again appear in the action of the narrative past this point. Love as a God has been removed from the stage of the *Vita Nuova*. Dante, working within the heritage of the troubadour tradition, has abolished the God of Love of troubadour mythology. In so doing he has made his lie a truer lie. Dante is the only one in the whole tradition to do this. And counting Petrarch as the last troubadour, that tradition, it should be remembered, is nearly three centuries long and is well cultivated. There would have been another way of handling an inherited mythology which needed to be squared with the truth: to treat it allegorically, to "undo" the literal sense in allegorical interpretation.[10] Dante did not choose that way. Nor did Plato, who rejected allegory as a means of reconciling an old mythology to his brave new world of reason. It is also a part of the same thing that Plato insisted that there is only one stage and that that is the stage of this life; that there is only one troupe of actors and that we are they. He felt, as a corollary to this, that the voice of the lyric poet is nearer to the truth than is the voice of the epic or tragic poet because that voice can be listened to as if it were acting on the real stage of this world. A poet speaking in the first person, as it were, in his own person, can be considered to be more responsible morally. Now Dante did not have a living contemporary epic or tragic tradition to reject. And in agreement with his age he did, of course, accept the allegorical interpretation of pagan mythology. That was an established practice; it was not of his doing nor was he the philosopher to question it. But the living tradition was a lyrical tradition. And Dante's poetry, all of it, is based on that tradition. It works in the first person.

Within that tradition, however, Dante does reject exactly that part of the inherited mythology which could prevent the action of love from being or appearing to be really on the stage of this life. With both Plato and Dante, of course, the stage of this life means a stage that is open at the top, that looks up to a transcendental God or Good who is always part of the action. On what a teleological cosmos will include or be transcended by, they in some essential sense agree. And that cosmos can no more admit the troubadour God of Love than it can the banqueting and jealous Gods of Homer. The epic Gods cannot be tolerated on the same stage (and there is only one) with the One who cannot be anything but the Good. Neither can the troubadour God of Love find any place on the same stage with the Christian God who is Himself Love. And Chapter XXV of the *Vita Nuova* eliminated the troubadour God. Henceforth—and I mean from here on to the last verse of the *Divine Comedy*—Dante is Plato's poet. He would not, I think, have been driven from the Republic, if the Republic were medieval and Christian. Henceforth, when Dante speaks of love (and in a sense he wrote of nothing else) it is always as a participation in that Love which moves the sun and all the stars. Love, says Dante in the *Vita Nuova*, is an accident in a substance. But our commentators do not tell us what we very much need to know, that this is a definition of love which both Augustine and Bernard of Clairvaux (to name only two) would have accepted as true of the only love they recognized in their philosophies, of that love which comes from God and is a gift of God and is more commonly known as Charity (*Caritas*). They so define Caritas as it is in man: an accident in a substance. Being a gift of God, it is on earth an accident. And there is no love that is not a gift of God, that is not a participation in the love of the Father for the Son and of the Son for the Father. Substantial love is God. *Deus caritas est.*[11]

Dante stands alone in the whole tradition. Lewis, in the volume I have mentioned, shows us what other poets were in the habit of doing.[12] They waited until the end, knowing all the while

that they were singing of a love which did not come from God
and could not return to God and face Him. In theory as well as
in practice, from Andreas Capellanus to Petrarch they played
truant from Reason—and then, in the end, they repented and
recanted. It is not a picture Plato would have liked.

I pass over the *Convivio* which is written after the *Vita Nuova*
and which is, beyond any question, a work in allegory. Dante
apparently lost interest in it and left it a mere fragment of what
he had intended.[13] And I come to the *Divine Comedy*. Now what
about the allegory here? And if Plato does not approve of allegory, could this be his poem?

The question is evidently tricky in this context. We must distinguish one kind of allegory from another. There is the allegory of interpretation in which the interpreter is not the one
who created the myth but only one who is reconciling that myth
to a truth or doctrine of which its maker often was quite un-
aware. The medieval interpretation of pagan mythology is the
familiar example. And that is the kind of allegory, of course,
which Plato rejected. There is on the other hand, that kind of
allegory, which is deliberately and intentionally woven into the
structure of the imaginative work itself. And the *Divine Comedy*
is evidently the case of the second.

If we were trying to see Dante as Plato's poet, then Plato's
opposition to allegory would inevitably lead us back to the
question of the allegory of the *Divine Comedy*. One thing, at
least, is clear. The vision of the *Divine Comedy* is, or means to
be, total vision. That is why it has so little of the quality of
medieval vision literature which, on the order of the *De con-
solatione philosophiae*, does deal in the kind of allegory that
is external. Such visions are had in an atmosphere of dream, they
are excuses for a didacticism which has little in common with the
Comedy. For the allegory of Dante's poem is only its way of
being complete vision. There is no key on the outside with
which to translate this poem to the truth of another system of
thought—the kind of allegory to which Plato would have ob-
jected. And if this poem needed to be so translated it would
mean that the myth of the *Divine Comedy* was not really on
speaking terms with the truth. But Dante's myth is supremely

according to the truth which he and his age recognized. It is no truancy from this life nor from the one struggle that counts. It only manages to stage more than this life by staging also the next which, for human souls, is the outcome of this one. And in the poem the voice of the poet speaks in the first person. The poet has moved himself on to the stage as a responsible actor. This poem, moreover, is not only open at the top toward the Good. It is literally suspended from it and no poem has ever kept the One and the Good so strictly in view from first to last. In its terza rima it even reflects the Trinity which is One and Three. And finally the stage of its action is also open to us. We are invited to participate through the character Dante. By keeping him as man (*homo viator*) the poem keeps the door open to us as well. One sees what it means to say that this is total vision. It is a literal truth. And if Plato had recognized as the truth what Dante embraced as the truth, and if he could have known Dante, he would surely have found in him *his* poet.

This may be about as far as it is profitable to try to take the idea of Dante as Plato's poet. The idea is, after all, only a way of looking at Dante. Another way equally as interesting would be to look in Dante for the poet of whom Plato would not have approved: to see, that is, in Dante's conception of the eternal world, the abyss which separates him from the Greek philosopher. We know full well that their idea of the nature of the world beyond change is not at all the same. In Dante's time not only is the primacy of the philosophy and the dialectic of Plato gone; but Plato's belief about the nature of that world beyond this world of change is also gone. Dante's treatment of what he has called his literal subject, the state of souls after death, would have shocked Plato were it intended as a representation of what *might* be true. And that it surely is. Of course, in the myth of the *Republic*, Er does come back from the other world with a report of certain experiences which would seem to be experiences of the senses. But then Er by a freak of fate was enjoying the special privilege of seeing as the living can see who are still a part of change. Later Aeneas too went in the body to the nether region and spoke to Dido and to his old father. But Dido and Anchises and what Er saw or what young Scipio sees in his

dream in Book VI of Cicero's *De re publica*, all are but the palest
shadows compared with what we meet in Dante's other world.
They are truly shades. Dante seems to have remembered the
quality of the ancient Hades and Elysian Fields when, up on
the mountain of Purgatory, he has Statius try to embrace Virgil
and Virgil say to him: "Friend, do not try; for you are a shade
and you see a shade in me." But even the casual reader of Dante's
poem knows that such a reminder of the unreality of the body
in the world beyond is rather the exception. He has too many
very clear memories of the exact opposite, of souls frozen in the
ice of lower Hell, and of Dante stumbling against one of them
in the dark; of Dante pulling the hair from the head of one
of them; of Ugolino gnawing at the skull and brain of his arch-
enemy; of Filippo Argenti being seized and ducked in the mud
of Styx. Or he remembers meeting old Brunetto Latini in Canto
XV of Hell; and we may recall Brunetto here in more detail and
let him represent the concrete reality of Dante's world beyond,
whether in Hell, or in Paradise where eagles and crosses and
ladders of pure light persuade our senses even as much as bodies
do in Hell.

In life Brunetto was a professor, a *litterato grande*. In Hell
he comes in company with a band of souls, all sodomites, running
naked now upon a desert plain where flakes of fire fall on them
slowly and relentlessly like snow in mountains when there is
no wind. Dante and Virgil stand on an embankment which pro-
tects them from the snow of fire. As he passes, Brunetto squints at
Dante like an old tailor into the eye of a needle, recognizes his
former pupil from Florence, and seizing him by the hem of his
garment cries: "Qual maraviglia!" And Dante reaching out to
touch the burned face before him, the better to make out the
features of that face, knows his teacher whom he has loved and
still loves and cries out in turn: "Are *you* here, Messir Brunetto?"

The symbolism and allegory of the poem, *homo viator* and the
sign in things, rest lightly here. Dante has said that the literal
meaning must come first and indeed it does with a force that
makes us forget the others. Here we see Brunetto as Brunetto
only, and Dante as Dante only, because each of them sees the
other in that way. Neither discovers man in general in the

other but only a certain very definite personal acquaintance.

Now it is this aspect of the poem, this first subject, that I mean to examine as myth in Dante. It is not the whole myth by any means, but it is perhaps the most striking among its several dimensions, and it is the first foundation of all of them. We are indeed a long way here from Plato. It was the faith of Socrates before he drank the poison that he would be quit of this body in death. His faith is in agreement with a position in philosophy according to which not even so much as the representation of a triangle gets into the eternal world of ideas. How now, in turn, do we account for Brunetto in Dante's philosophy? Vico would have talked of the unreflective primitive mind here, no doubt— but, for Dante, Vico no longer satisfies our sense of what the truth is concerning Dante. Dante, as we have seen, was conscious enough of his art to lay down a law for poets. Poets are responsible to the truth. May it not seem then that Dante has taken liberties here as mythmaker—liberties which Reason or Philosophy or the Faith could not have approved and that must accordingly be translated to other terms? Not at all. And in the letter to Can Grande, Dante has not even felt the need of justifying this aspect of his vision; on the contrary, he takes it most for granted. It is simply his intention, his first intention, to show the state of souls after death. Just that. No further comment.

We come thus to our question paralleling the one which may be addressed to Plato the philosopher. What is the position of this myth within Dante's philosophy; or, as we have agreed that we must call it, his faith? Here we venture out on our own. Dante did not say. Apparently he anticipated no objections to this way of seeing in the world beyond. And the reason why he did not is, I think, not far to seek. Indeed we have already touched on it. It has to do with that point which Augustine could not find in the philosophy of the Platonists: the Incarnation. For it is God in man, it is the Word made flesh and dwelling in us, which supports Dante's conception of the state of the soul after death. An unphilosophical Jehovah and the direct creation of the body of Adam can, of course, be another; for according to a well-known tenet of the faith, what God has created directly (that is, in the case of Adam, the flesh as well as the soul)

can never perish. But the truth of that too is finally proved by
an Incarnation and a Resurrection. It was that total event which
so sanctified the human body that a philosophical poet could
find our body in the eternal world beyond, and find it there in
all reality—find it there before it could really be there, for the
day of our Resurrection is not yet come when Dante visits the
three realms beyond. But that precisely is the liberty to be
granted to the maker of the myth. Thus Dante is able to build
on something in his philosophy which Plato did not admit in
his; and it is something rich in possibilities for a poet—how rich
one only knows who has seen that other world with Dante, a
world more real than this. Dante enjoys another great advantage
important to a poet. He can count on all his readers to agree with
him. Did they not all believe that one day they would have
their bodies (glorified) after death? That being true according
to the truth that is revealed, why then through myth may we
not see the body there already? And if the body, why not a
very concrete and most tangible world that goes, or seems to
go, with the body? *Verbum caro factum est* will support a
very great deal.

One day, according to the faith, the whole man, body and
soul, will participate in beatitude or damnation. Here then we
have a measure of the margin between the faith and the myth.
The myth is only saying: "If one day, why not now?"

But if that is the article of faith which can support what the
poet sees beyond, what of the kind of seeing that accompanies
and must accompany it to have it so? Dante, after all, sees not
only human souls, but in the end sees God. And he sees God
as Plato never would. Again the answer is not hard to find. We
turn to a famous passage in the first Pauline epistle to the Corinthians:

> When I was a child, I spake as a child, I understood as a child, I
> thought as a child; but when I became a man I put away childish
> things. For now we see through a glass, darkly; but then face to
> face: now I know in part; but then shall I know even as also I am
> known.

One day, that is, we shall see, face to face, God and God's
justice. After death, according to the faith, we are really to see

even as Dante sees in myth. And then, when the Last Day has come, we are to have our bodies (glorified) and the glorified eyes of our bodies and we are to see as we have seen on earth— only better. See then face to face; and if then, why not now? The question gives the position of Dante's myth within his philosophy.

But the question in the negative may seem to beg the question. Might one not also ask why wish to see face to face? The question, I know, seems most naïve; but we are deliberately pushing it for what it may yield. Put thus in the positive, the question asks, in other words, not only why this particular myth within the faith, but why any myth at all within the faith? Here I am relieved of the burden of an answer on my own. Dante makes it and it is in striking agreement with Plato. Socrates in the *Phaedo* and Plato elsewhere found the value of myth to be that it orders our hopes and fears, that it sets us right with the world. The myth, the right myth, the true lie, is something that we should sing over and over to ourselves. Now, in his *De vulgari eloquentia* we find that Dante distinguishes three subject matters for poetry.[14] (Dante does not theorize about myth as such.) The first two of these are arms or martial exploits, and secondly, love of woman. But these subjects, he says, are not his. His is a third, to which he gives the name in Latin of *directio voluntatis* which must mean both the *rightness* and the *righting* of the will. His song is a song to the will of man directing it to the Good. Would not Plato have agreed in this use of myth and poetry? Even as Dante appears to have agreed with him that there is only one stage in this life and that all things must find their place thereon in their right order. They must be ordered to the good. Any action that does not so involve them is false. In a strictly teleological cosmos both myth and poetry must have a use and that use cannot be very different. Plato and Dante agree on what it is. It is the regulation of the will of man. What their myth sees it is right that men should see and good that they should see. This is a use for art which even Tolstoi would not have condemned.

But it is no shallow didacticism and it is no mere literary allegory that will touch the will of man. All the powers of the mythopœic fancy and what we have since called the creative imagination are required. Plato and Dante would agree on that too. It is seeing that directs the will. We must really see.

* * *

But somehow for us the argument is not yet complete. The whole man, or perhaps it is the modern man in us, demands a further extension of this subject and puts another question. We want to know not *why* so much as *how*. How, that is, are we moderns, how is our modern mind, to understand the way of seeing that we find in Plato's myth and Dante's poetry? How is it possible to see Brunetto Latini as he is seen by Dante?

It may be that one finds no problem here at all. We readily make the assumption of the creative imagination and we stand always ready to answer that this seeing is the peculiar power of great poets and let it go at that. But I suspect that we are readier to let it go at that because we do not quite understand. Or maybe we understand less about it than Dante or Plato did and hence we make a problem of what was for them no problem. However that may be, one thing is clear: our modern mind is disinclined to face the myth directly. We face it historically and talk about what man once believed. We stand ready, that is, to do with history what other ages did with allegory. For history, like allegory, converts to other terms and other truths. Mythology becomes comparative mythology. But if we face the myth directly we are, I fear, somewhat uneasy. It is something like facing man directly. I wonder really if we are not already beyond understanding? For us there is no longer any identity of thought and being. What the artist creates exists in an illusory space which a science of aesthetics is supposed to be able to deal with. The problem is of the Renaissance. And it is also of the Renaissance (and not at all unrelated) that our faith in the ability of the word to contain a changeless truth continues to diminish until we find it hard and some of us find it intolerable to see things timelessly. When we shall have completely lost the belief in the possibility of transcending the world of change which is the world of history, then we shall have lost a space, a dimension, which is needed not only by religion and metaphysics

but by myth and poetry as well. When there is no transcendence
of change, no escape from the flux of things, how can we have
anything but history? (I will not press the question, that being
true, how we can have history either!) How, in short, can the
word any longer hold truth as it did for Plato and for Dante?
It is otherwise with our faith in the mathematical symbol. But
in the word the possibility of metaphysical and mythical "space"
is fast vanishing. Shall we dare then to face the myth directly
and pretend to understand? (These are questions which a teacher
of Dante has to face if he would teach Dante as anything but
an historical document.)

Sometimes we put the burden of it all on the maker of the
myth. We put it off on Dante, say, and grow mystical about
him. No one today really believes, I suppose, that Dante actually
went to the other world. But neither would Thomas Aquinas
have believed that, had he been able to read the poem. Only
some readers today speak from a position but slightly less naïve
and say that Dante himself must have believed that he had really
been to the world beyond and that he wrote of what must have
been for him a real experience. And in answer to the question
of how he might have thought he got there, these readers point
to miraculous powers and to the grace of God through whom
all things are possible. Now it is true that Dante might have
made any one of several answers. In a world in which the super-
natural may at any time break through the natural and the miracle occur, almost anything can happen. At least there is no saying what may not happen even in the category of knowledge.

The poem itself is built on the pattern of this possibility of
divine grace and divine inspiration. But to attribute to a critical
and reflective Dante the belief that he was another Aeneas or
another St. Paul is simply to unload on him our own disinclina-
tion to face the myth directly and to understand it. The power
to see in words as he saw may indeed come ultimately from God.
We do not understand the miracle of inspiration any better than
Plato did or Dante. But in view of the passage I have quoted
from the letter to Can Grande and the remarks from the *De
vulgari eloquentia*, evidence enough of a Dante able to reason
about his myth as his and as a poem, I think that with him we

had better stop talking Vico's primitivism. And the more so if
it is true that Dante is Plato's poet, if he is truly the poet responsible for his myth according to the truth. Dante had his
eyes open. And it is simply up to us to straighten ourselves out
on this matter and to face the myth as myth and try to understand.

But there are myths and myths as any one soon realizes who
will read the account of the creation in Ovid's *Metamorphoses*[15]
and then read Genesis. If the reader will agree to this, that there
is a sharp line dividing Ovid and Genesis according to a fundamental quality in their way of seeing what is seen; and if we then
ask on which side of this line we shall put Plato and Dante, the
answer is surely on the side of Genesis. Genesis indeed can make
us better aware of a certain quality of vision in both Plato's myth
and Dante's poem. Not that the *Comedy* does not contain myths
of the quality of Ovid's. Dante, after all, draws heavily on an
ancient literary mythology and, unlike Plato and the author of
Genesis, is working in a conscious literary tradition. The more
remarkable then that we do find Genesis and Plato in him. But
I shall probably express myself more clearly on the point I wish
to make here if I say that the way in which Dante discovers and
sees Brunetto Latini in Hell has something fundamental and
categorical in common with the way Genesis finds and sees
God. And if this prove true to the reader's feeling in the matter,
then we are in a position to observe that at the bottom of Dante's
poetry (of his literal subject, at least, "the state of souls after
death") there is an imagination at work which is more mythical
than poetic.

In the beginning God created the heaven and the earth. And the
earth was without form and void; and darkness was upon the face of
the deep. And the Spirit of God moved upon the face of the waters.

That is not a text that needs quoting. Neither will I take time
to look at Brunetto Latini again. My question is this: how, from
a human point of view, shall we understand this kind of seeing,
this kind of knowing? What is the psychology of it? If we can
answer that question for Genesis, we shall have answered it for
Dante and Plato. But neither Dante nor Plato, as I have said,

show the least concern for the question. For them there was still the space, the transcendent space, within which such things could be and could be seen. Even so, they are mysterious. But suppose we insist. Let us address our question to the text of Genesis a little further on, just after Adam and Eve have eaten the forbidden fruit:

> And the eyes of them both were opened and they knew that they were naked; and they sewed fig leaves together, and made themselves aprons. And they heard the voice of the Lord God walking in the garden in the cool of the day: and Adam and his wife hid themselves.

Poetry will not always translate. Myth sometimes will. But our question is: How can the author of Genesis lay claim to this kind of knowledge? How can he pretend to be present, even in the mind, at such a scene as this? If these things are to be believed, what is our belief to rest on? That is, what does it rest on in the author of Genesis? The question concerns Dante and Brunetto as much as Genesis and God. We can answer by analogy. How can Dante pretend to knowledge of the state of souls after death? In the same way that the author of Genesis has knowledge of the creation. He was probably unreflective about his myth and we have seen that Dante was reflective. But even Dante in his reasoned letter to Can Grande neglects the *how* of it. It is no more a question for him than it was for the other or for Plato. The question, let me repeat, is ours.

And so, if we go beyond analogies, we shall have to answer that this is faith writing. This is a kind of knowing and seeing which begins as a movement of faith and culminates in vision. It is as though faith moved first and then the eye could see. In the myths of Plato it is not otherwise. Plato, even, being a philosopher, seems to be aware of this. And he smiles down upon the thing. The author of Genesis and Dante evidently do not smile.

Would it not have been simpler, one may ask, to have said right off that we were talking of religious myth? Perhaps. Only just what that would have explained about Brunetto Latini in Hell is not clear. It is commonly said that Dante put his enemies in Hell. And indeed he did. But to put it that way is only another

way out of facing the myth directly. Again that puts the problem
on Dante and puts it in terms which our shifting relativistic
modern mind is all too ready to take refuge in. For it needs be
said that Dante put his friends in Hell too. There is no reason
at all to believe that Dante did not love Brunetto as he might have
loved a father. There is every reason to believe that, had it
depended on him, Dante would have had Brunetto in Paradise.
But what I am trying to account for (and what the term religious myth might not account for in this case) is this: *that
it does not depend on Dante*. This is a vision, not of things as
we should wish them to be, but of things as they are. These are
things which, even before they are seen, are submitted to the
lap of God; and because of this, when they are seen, they are
objective. They do not stand in illusory space. They stand in
a space that God sees. To remember St. Paul, they are known
even as we are known. Does the author of Genesis want God to
create beasts and man on the sixth day rather than another? Or
does God walk in the garden in the cool of the evening because
the author likes the idea? Again we answer question with question. But sometimes that is the best way—or perhaps the only
way.

As for Dante, I am here talking about a quality of vision which
becomes a pervading quality of his poetry. To anyone who
knows his poem well it amounts to a steady feeling that somehow beyond his words there is a reality which would remain
even if the words were taken away. And I am looking for a
formula which will account psychologically for this quality in
Dante. I think we had one back along our path when we talked
of Aquinas and the position of philosophy in the Middle Ages.
It was a well-worn formula which one recognized immediately:
fides quaerens intellectum, faith seeking understanding. Or there
is another version: *praecedit fides, sequitur intellectus*, faith goes
ahead, understanding follows. Now if I may be allowed to alter
these formulae ever so little, we shall have one to account for
the quality I speak of in Dante's poem. I would suggest: *fides
quaerens visionem; praecedit fides, sequitur visio*. And this, I sub-
mit, fits not only a quality in Dante but the myth of Genesis
and Plato's myth. There may be others that one would want to

add to the list. But I suspect they are not many. There are no others in Italian literature either before or after Dante. Neither in Petrarch nor in Tasso nor in Leopardi does faith move before the tongue moves or the eye sees. Petrarch's space of imagination is already a space of illusion. He and the others belong to the Renaissance and aesthetics can perhaps claim to deal with them. But aesthetics as the science of the beautiful can never deal with Plato's myth or Genesis or Dante's poem. For they aim neither at beauty (not first of all) nor illusion. Theirs is a vision of an objective order of things in its goodness and its rightness. And for them anything short of this were ugliness.

Notes

1. Wicksteed (in *The Latin Works of Dante*, Temple Classics Edition, London, 1940, p. 363) has on this quotation by Dante the following note: "The passage of the *Metaphysics* referred to occurs at the end of the first chapter of the book, known as 'Little Alpha,' which is numbered in the Latin translations as Book II. The form in which Dante cites it is '*Sicut res se habet ad esse, sic se habet ad veritatem,*' which does not correspond with either of the versions current in his time. Albertus Magnus, however, says in his paraphrase (II, 4), 'unumquodque sicut se habet ad esse, ita se habet ad veritatem,' and no doubt this is the source of Dante's phrase."

2. This is true, even when the poem seems to call itself a vision, as in *Paradiso* XXXIII, 62: "chè quasi tutta cessa mia visione." Here, as elsewhere (*Paradiso* XIV, 49; *Paradiso* XVII, 128), the word means "a seeing" or "that which is seen," without denying the literal reality of the journey beyond.

3. *Soliloquies* II, 10 (PL 32, 895).

4. The reader, from this point on (in so far as Plato is considered) is referred to the essay by Ludwig Edelstein, "The Function of the Myth in Plato's Philosophy," which appeared together with the main part of the present chapter as a companion article in the *Journal of the History of Ideas* X, 463 ff.

5. *Confessions* VII, ix.

6. *Summa contra Gentiles* IV, 1.

7. A more extensive discussion of this particular point, and the strategy of it in the *Vita Nuova*, may be seen in the author's *Essay*, p. 74 ff.

8. *The Allegory of Love* (Oxford, 1936), 47–48.

9. *Republic* II, 378.

10. As is done in the *Convivio*, with an "allegory of poets." *See* Appendix *infra*.

11. *See* the author's *Essay,* p. 75 and *passim.*
12. Lewis, *op. cit.,* p. 43 *circa.*
13. *See* Appendix *infra.*
14. II, II, 9.
15. *Metamorphoses,* I, 1.

Appendix

The Two Kinds of Allegory

In his *Convivio* Dante recognizes two kinds of allegory: an "allegory of poets" and an "allegory of theologians." And in the interpretation of his own poems in that work he declares that he intends to follow the allegory of poets, for the reason that the poems were composed after that manner of allegory.

It is well to recall that there is an unfortunate lacuna in the text of the *Convivio* at just this most interesting point, with the result that those words which defined the literal sense, as distinguished from the allegorical, are missing. But no one who knows the general argument of the whole work will, I think, make serious objection to the way the editors of the accepted critical text have filled the lacuna.

The passage in question, patched by them, reads as follows:

> Dico che, sì come nel primo capitolo è narrato, questa sposizione conviene essere literale e allegorica. E a ciò dare a intendere, si vuol sapere che le scritture si possono intendere e deonsi esponere mas-

simamente per quattro sensi. L'uno si chiama litterale [e questo è quello che non si stende più oltre la lettera de le parole fittizie, sì come sono le favole de li poeti. L'altro si chiama allegorico] e questo è quello che si nasconde sotto'l manto di queste favole, ed è una veritade ascosa sotto bella menzogna: sì come quando dice Ovidio che Orfeo facea con la cetera mansuete le fiere, e li arbori e le pietre a sè muovere; che vuol dire che lo savio uomo con lo strumento de la sua voce fa[r]ia mansuescere e umiliare li crudeli cuori, e fa[r]ia muovere a la sua volontade coloro che non hanno vita di scienza e d'arte: e coloro che non hanno vita ragionevole alcuna sono quasi come pietre. E perchè questo nascondimento fosse trovato per li savi, nel penultimo trattato si mosterrà. Veramente li teologi questo senso prendono altrimenti che li poeti; ma però che mia intenzione è qui lo modo de li poeti seguitare, prendo lo senso allegorico secondo che per li poeti è usato.[1]

I say that, as is narrated in the first chapter, this exposition is to be both literal and allegorical. And to make this clear, one should know that writing can be understood and must be explained mainly in four senses. One is called the literal [and this is the sense that does not go beyond the letter of the fictive words, as are the fables of the poets. The other is called allegorical], and this is the sense that is hidden under the cloak of these fables, and it is a truth hidden under the beautiful lie; as when Ovid says that Orpheus tamed the wild beasts with his zither and caused the trees and the stones to come to him; which signifies that the wise man with the instrument of his voice would make cruel hearts gentle and humble, and would make those who do not live in science and art do his will; and those who have no kind of life of reason in them are as stones. And the reason why this concealment was devised by wise men will be shown in the next to the last treatise. It is true that theologians understand this sense otherwise than do the poets; but since it is my intention here to follow after the manner of the poets, I take the allegorical sense as the poets are wont to take it.

Dante goes on here to distinguish the customary third and fourth senses, the moral and the anagogical. However, in illustration of these no example from "the poets" is given. For both senses, the example in illustration is taken from Holy Scripture. It is, however, evident from the closing words of the chapter that in the exposition of the poems of the *Convivio*, the third and fourth senses will have only an incidental interest and that the poet is to concern himself mainly with the first two.[2]

It was no doubt inevitable that the conception of allegory

which Dante here calls the allegory of poets should come to be identified with the allegory of the *Divine Comedy*. This, after all, is a formulation of the matter of allegory by Dante himself. It distinguishes an allegory of poets from an allegory of theologians. Now poets create and theologians only interpret. And, if we must choose between Dante as theologian and Dante as poet, then, I suppose, we take the poet.[3] For the *Divine Comedy*, all are agreed, is the work of a poet, is a poem. Why, then, would its allegory not be allegory as the poets understood it— that is, as Dante, in the *Convivio*, says the poets understood it? Surely the allegory of the *Comedy* is the allegory of poets in which the first and literal sense is a fiction and the second or allegorical sense is the true one.[4]

Indeed, with some Dante scholars, so strong has the persuasion been that such a view of the allegory of the *Divine Comedy* is the correct one that it has brought them to question the authorship of the famous letter to Can Grande.[5] This, in all consistency, was bound to occur. For the Letter, in pointing out the allegory of the *Commedia*, speaks in its turn of the usual four senses. But the example of allegory which it gives is not taken from Ovid nor indeed from the work of any poet. Let us consider this famous and familiar passage:

Ad evidentiam itaque dicendorum sciendum est quod istius operis non est simplex sensus, ymo dici potest polisemos, hoc est plurium sensuum; nam primus sensus est qui habetur per litteram, alius est qui habetur per significata per litteram. Et primus dicitur litteralis, secundus vero allegoricus sive moralis sive anagogicus. Qui modus tractandi, ut melius pateat, potest considerari in hiis versibus: "In exitu Israel de Egypto, domus Iacob ed populo barbaro, facta est Iudea sanctificatio eius, Israel potestas eius." Nam si ad litteram solam inspiciamus, significatur nobis exitus filiorum Israel de Egypto, tempore Moysis; si ad allegoriam, nobis significatur nostra redemptio facta per Christum; si ad moralem sensum significatur nobis conversio anime de luctu et miseria peccati ad statum gratie: si ad anagogicum, significatur exitus anime sancte ab huius corruptionis servitute ad eterne glorie libertatem. Et quanquam isti sensus mistici variis appellentur nominibus, generaliter omnes dici possunt allegorici, cum sint a litterali sive historiali diversi. Nam allegoria dicitur ab "alleon" grece, quod in latinum dicitur "alienum," sive "diversum."[6]

To elucidate, then, what we have to say, be it known that the sense of this work is not simple, but on the contrary it may be called polysemous, that is to say, "of more senses than one"; for it is one sense that we get through the letter, and another which we get through the thing the letter signifies; and the first is called literal, but the second allegorical or mystic. And this mode of treatment, for its better manifestation, may be considered in this verse: "When Israel came out of Egypt, and the house of Jacob from a people of strange speech, Judaea became his sanctification, Israel his power." For if we inspect the letter alone, the departure of the children of Israel from Egypt in the time of Moses is presented to us; if the allegory, our redemption wrought by Christ; if the moral sense, the conversion of the soul from the grief and misery of sin to the state of grace is presented to us; if the anagogical, the departure of the holy soul from the slavery of this corruption to the liberty of eternal glory is presented to us. And although these mystic senses have each their special denominations, they may all in general be called allegorical, since they differ from the literal and historical. Now allegory is so called from "alleon" in Greek, which means in Latin "alieum" or "diversum."

and the Letter continues directly as follows:

Hiis visis, manifestum est quod duplex oportet esse subiectum, circa quod currant alterni sensus. Et ideo videndum est de subiecto huius operis, prout ad litteram accipitur; deinde de subiecto, prout allegorice sententiatur. Est ergo subiectum totius operis, litteraliter tantum accepti, status animarum post mortem simpliciter sumptus; nam de illo et circa illum totius operis versatur processus. Si vero accipiatur opus allegorice, subiectum est homo prout merendo et demerendo per arbitrii libertatem iustitie premiandi et puniendi obnoxius est.

When we understand this we see clearly that the subject round which the alternative senses play must be twofold. And we must therefore consider the subject of this work as literally understood, and then its subject as allegorically intended. The subject of the whole work, then, taken in the literal sense only is "the state of souls after death" without qualification, for the whole progress of the work hinges on it and about it. Whereas if the work be taken allegorically, the subject is "man as by good or ill deserts, in the exercise of the freedom of his choice, he becomes liable to rewarding or punishing justice."

Now this, to return to the distinction made in the *Convivio*, is beyond the shadow of a doubt, the "allegory of theologians."

It is their kind of allegory not only because Holy Scripture is cited to illustrate it, but because since Scripture is cited, the first or literal sense cannot be fictive but must be true and, in this instance, historical. The effects of Orpheus' music on beasts and stones may be a poet's invention, setting forth under a veil of fiction some hidden truth, but the Exodus is no poet's invention.

All medievalists are familiar with the classical statement of the "allegory of theologians" as given by St. Thomas Aquinas toward the beginning of the *Summa Theologica:*

> Auctor Sacrae Scripturae est Deus, in cuius potestate est ut non solum voces ad significandum accommodet, quod etiam homo facere potest, sed etiam res ipsas. Et ideo cum in omnibus scientiis voces significent, hoc habet proprium ista scientia, quod ipsae res significatae per voces, etiam significant aliquid. Illa ergo prima significatio, qua voces significant res, pertinet ad primum sensum, qui est sensus historicus vel litteralis. Illa vero significatio qua res significatae per voces, iterum res alias significant, dicitur sensus spiritualis, qui super litteralem fundatur et eum supponit.[7]

> The author of Holy Scripture is God, in whose power it is to signify His meaning, not by words only (as man also can do) but also by things themselves. So, whereas in every other science things are signified by words, this science has the property that the things signified by the words have themselves also a signification. Therefore that first signification whereby words signify things belongs to the first sense, the historical or literal. That signification whereby things signified by words have themselves also a signification is called the spiritual sense, which is based on the literal and presupposes it.

St. Thomas goes on to subdivide the second or spiritual sense into the usual three: the allegorical, the moral, and the anagogical. But in his first division into two he has made the fundamental distinction, which St. Augustine expressed in terms of one meaning which is *in verbis* and another meaning which is *in facto.*[8] And, in reading his words, one may surely recall Dante's in the Letter: "nam primus sensus est qui habetur per litteram, alius est qui habetur per significata per litteram."

An allegory of poets and an allegory of theologians: the Letter to Can Grande does not make the distinction. The Letter is speaking of the way in which a poem is to be understood. And in choosing its example of allegory from Holy Scripture, the Letter is clearly looking to the kind of allegory which is the allegory of theologians; and is thus pointing to a poem in which the first and literal sense is to be taken as the first and literal sense of Holy Scripture is taken, namely as an historical sense.[9] The well-known jingle on the four senses began, one recalls, "Littera *gesta* docet. . ."

But, before going further, let us ask if this matter can have more than antiquarian interest. When we read the *Divine Comedy* today, does it matter, really, whether we take its first meaning to be historical or fictive, since in either case we must enter into that willing suspension of disbelief required in the reading of any poem?

Indeed, it happens to matter very much, because with this poem it is not a question of one meaning but of two meanings; and the nature of the first meaning will necessarily determine the nature of the second—will say how we shall look for the second. In the case of a fictive first meaning, as in the "allegory of poets," interpretation will invariably speak in terms of an outer and an inner meaning, of a second meaning which is conveyed but also, in some way, deliberately concealed under the "shell" or the "bark" or the "veil" of an outer fictive meaning. This allegory of the poets, as Dante presents it in the *Convivio*, is essentially an allegory of "this for that," of "this figuration in order to give (and also to conceal) that meaning." Orpheus and the effects of his music yield the meaning that a wise man can tame cruel hearts. It should be noted that here we are not concerned with allegory as expressed in a personification, but of an allegory of action, of event.

But the kind of allegory to which the example from Scriptures given in the Letter to Can Grande points is not an allegory of "this for that," but an allegory of "this *and* that," of this sense plus that sense. The verse in Scripture which says "When Israel went out of Egypt," has its first meaning in denoting a real historical event; and it has its second meaning because that historical event itself, having the Author that it had, can signify yet another event: our Redemption through Christ. Its first meaning is a meaning *in verbis;* its other meaning is a meaning *in facto,* in the event itself. The words have a real meaning in pointing to a real event; the event, in its turn, has meaning because events wrought by God are themselves as words yielding a meaning, a higher and spiritual sense.

But there was a further point about this kind of allegory of Scriptures: it was generally agreed that while the first literal meaning would always be there, *in verbis,*[10] the second or spiritual meaning was not always to be found in all the things and events that the words pointed to. Some events yielded the second meaning, some did not. And it is this fact which best shows that the literal historical meaning of Scriptures was not necessarily a sense in the service of another sense, not therefore a matter of "this for that." It is this that matters most in the interpretation of the *Divine Comedy.*

The crux of the matter, then, is this: If we take the allegory of the *Divine Comedy* to be the allegory of poets (as Dante understood that allegory in the *Convivio*) then we shall be taking it as a construction in which the literal sense ought always to be expected to yield another sense because the literal is only a fiction devised to express a second meaning. In this view the first meaning, if it does not give another, true meaning, has no excuse for being. Whereas, if we take the allegory of the *Divine Comedy* to be the allegory of theologians, we shall expect to find in the poem a first literal meaning presented as a meaning which is not fictive but true, because the words which give that meaning point to events which are seen as historically true. And we shall see these events themselves reflecting a second meaning because their author, who is God, can use events as men use words. *But,* we shall not demand at every moment that the event signified by the words be in its turn as a word, because this is not the case in Holy Scripture.[11]

*   *   *

One should have no difficulty in making the choice. The allegory of the *Divine Comedy* is so clearly the "allegory of theologians" (as the Letter to Can Grande by its example says it is) that one may only wonder at the continuing efforts made to see it as the "allegory of poets." What indeed increases the wonder at this effort is that every attempt to treat the first meaning of the poem as a fiction devised to convey a true but hidden meaning has been such a clear demonstration of how a poem may be forced to meanings that it cannot possibly bear as a poem.[12]

It seems necessary to illustrate the matter briefly with a single and obvious example. All readers of the *Comedy*, whatever their allegorical credo, must recognize that Virgil, for instance, if he be taken statically, in isolation from the action of the poem, had and has, as the poem would see him, a real historical existence. He was a living man and he is now a soul dwelling in Limbo. Standing alone, he would have no other, no second meaning, at all. It is by having a role in the action of the poem that Virgil takes on a second meaning. And it is at this point that the view one holds of the nature of the first meaning begins to matter. For if this is the allegory of poets, then what Virgil does, like what Orpheus does, is a fiction devised to convey a hidden meaning which it ought to convey all the time, since only by conveying that other meaning is what he does justified at all. Instead, if this action is allegory as theologians take it, then this action must always have a literal sense which is historical and no fiction; and thus Virgil's deeds as part of the whole action may, in their turn, be as words signifying other things; but they do not have to do this all the time, because, being historical, those deeds exist simply in their own right.

But can we hesitate in such a choice? Is it not clear that Virgil can not and does not always speak and act as Reason, with a capital initial, and that to try to make him do this is to try to rewrite the poem according to a conception of allegory which the poem does not bear within itself?

If, then, the allegory of the *Divine Comedy* is the allegory of theologians, if it is an allegory of "this and that," if its allegory may be seen in terms of a first meaning which is *in verbis* and of another meaning which is *in facto*, what is the main outline of its allegorical structure?

In the simplest and briefest possible statement it is this: the journey to God of a man through three realms of the world

beyond this life is what is given by the literal meaning. It points
to the event. The event is that journey to God through the world
beyond. "Littera *gesta* docet." The words of the poem have their
first meaning in signifying that event, just as the verse of
Psalms had its first meaning in signifying the historical event of
the Exodus.

And then just as the event of the Exodus, being wrought by
God, can give in turn a meaning, namely, our Redemption
through Christ; so, in the event of this journey through the
world beyond (an event which, as the poem sees it, is also
wrought by God) we see the reflection of other meanings. These,
in the poem, are the various reflections of man's journey to his
proper end, not in the life after death, but here in this life, as that
journey was conceived possible in Dante's day—and not only
in Dante's day. The main allegory of the *Divine Comedy* is thus
an allegory of action, of event, an event given by words which
in its turn reflects, (*in facto*), another event. Both are journeys
to God.[13]

*   *   *

What, then, of the *Convivio?* Does not its "allegory of poets"
contradict this "allegory of theologians" in the later work? It
does, if a poet must always use one kind of allegory and may
not try one in one work and one in another. But shall we not
simply face this fact? And shall we not recognize that in this
sense the *Convivio* contradicts not only the *Divine Comedy* in
its allegory, but also the *Vita Nuova* where there is no allegory.[14]
The *Convivio* is Dante's attempt to use the "allegory of poets."
And to have that kind of allegory and the kind of figure that
could have a role in it—to have a Lady Philosophy who was an
allegory of poets—he was obliged to rob the "donna pietosa"
of the *Vita Nuova* of all real existence. And in doing this he
contradicted the *Vita Nuova.*

The *Convivio* is a fragment. We do not know why Dante gave
up the work before it was hardly under way. We do not know.
We are, therefore, free to speculate. I venture to do so, and
suggest that Dante abandoned the *Convivio* because he came to

see that in choosing to build this work according to the allegory
of poets, he had ventured down a false way; that he came to
realize that a poet could not be a poet of rectitude and work
with an allegory whose first meaning was a disembodied fiction.

St. Gregory, in the Proem to his Exposition of the Song of
Songs, says: "Allegoria enim animae longe a Deo positae quasi
quamdam machinam facit ut per illam levetur ad Deum" [15]
and the Letter to Can Grande declares that the end of the whole
Comedy is "to remove those living in this life from the state of
misery and lead them to the state of felicity." A poet of rectitude
is one who is interested in directing the will of men to God. But a
disembodied Lady Philosophy is not a *machina* which can bear
the weight of lifting man to God because, in her, man finds no
part of his own weight. Lady Philosophy did not, does not, will
not, exist in the flesh. As she is constructed in the *Convivio* she
comes to stand for Sapientia, for created Sapientia standing in
analogy to uncreated Sapientia Which is the Word.[16] Even so,
she is word without flesh. And only the word made flesh can
lift man to God. If the allegory of a Christian poet of rectitude
is to support any weight, it will be grounded in the flesh, which
means grounded in history—and will lift up from there. In
short, the trouble with Lady Philosophy was the trouble which
Augustine found with the Platonists: "But that the Word was
made flesh and dwelt among us I did not read there." [17]

Dante, then, abandons Lady Philosophy and returns to Beatrice.
But now the way to God must be made open to all men: he
constructs an allegory, a *machina*, that is, in which an historical
Virgil, an historical Beatrice, and an historical Bernard replace
that Lady in an action which is given, in its first sense, not as
a beautiful fiction but as a real, historical event, an event remembered by one who was, as a verse of the poem says, the
scribe of it.[18] Historical and, by a Christian standard, beautiful [19]
as an allegory because bearing within it the reflection of the
true way to God in this life—a way given and supported by the
Word made flesh. With its first meaning as an historical meaning,
the allegory of the *Divine Comedy* is grounded in the mystery
of the Incarnation.[20]

In his commentary on the poem written some half century after the poet's death, Benvenuto da Imola would seem to understand the allegory of the *Divine Comedy* to be the "allegory of theologians." To make clear to some doubting reader the concept by which Beatrice has a second meaning, he points to Rachel in Holy Scripture:

> Nec videatur tibi indignum, lector, quod Beatrix mulier carnea accipiatur a Dante pro sacra theologia. Nonne Rachel secundum historicam veritatem fuit pulcra uxor Jacob summe amata ab eo, pro qua habenda custodivit oves per XIIII annos, et tamen anagogice figurat vitam contemplativam, quam Jacob mirabiliter amavit? Et si dicis: non credo quod Beatrix vel Rachel sumantur unquam spiritualiter, dicam quod contra negantes principia non est amplius disputandum. Si enim vis intelligere opus istius autoris, oportet concedere quod ipse loquatur catholice tamquam perfectus christianus, et qui semper et ubique conatur ostendere se christianum.[21]

> Let it not seem improper to you, reader, that Beatrice, a woman of flesh, should be taken by Dante as sacred Theology. Was not Rachel, according to historical truth, the beautiful wife of Jacob, loved exceedingly by him, to win whom he tended the sheep for fourteen years, and yet she figures the contemplative life which Jacob loved marvelously well? And if you say, I do not believe that Beatrice or Rachel ever had such spiritual meanings, then I say that against those who deny first principles there is no further disputing. For if you wish to understand the work of this writer, it is necessary to concede that he speaks in a catholic way as a perfect Christian and who always and everywhere strives to show himself a Christian.

Dr. Edward Moore once pointed, in a footnote, to these remarks by the early commentator and smiled at them as words that throw "a curious light on the logical processes of Benvenuto's mind." [22] But Benvenuto's words have, I think, a way of smiling back. And to make their smile more apparent to a modern reader one might transpose them so:

> Let it not seem improper to you, reader, that this journey of a living man into the world beyond is presented to you in its first sense as literally and historically true. And if you say: "I do not believe that Dante ever went to the other world," then I say that with those who deny what a poem asks be granted, there is no further disputing.

Notes to Appendix

1. *Convivio*, II, i, 2-4, in the standard edition with commentary by G. Busnelli and G. Vandelli (Florence, 1934). Concerning the lacuna and the reasons for filling it as this has been done (words in brackets in the passage above) *see* their notes to the passage, Vol. I, pp. 96-97 and 240-242. The "penultimo trattato" where Dante promises to explain the reason for the "allegory of poets" was, alas, never written.

2. *Convivio*, II, i, 15: "Io adunque, per queste ragioni, tuttavia sopra ciascuna canzone ragionerò prima la litterale sentenza, e appresso di quella ragionerò la sua allegoria, cioè la nascosa veritate; e talvolta de li altri sensi toccherò incidentemente, come a luogo e tempo si converrà."

3. One recalls, of course, that Boccaccio and many others have preferred the theologian. On Dante as theologian one may now see E. R. Curtius, *Europäische Literatur und lateinische Mittelalter* (Bern, 1948), pp. 219 ff. To see the poet as "theologian" is to see him essentially as one who constructs an "allegory of poets," hiding under a veil the truths of theology—a view which has a long history in Dante interpretation.

4. By no means all commentators of the poem who discuss this matter have faced the necessity of making a choice between the two kinds of allegory distinguished by Dante. More often than not, even in a discussion of the two kinds, they have preferred to leave the matter vague as regards the *Divine Comedy*. *See*, for example, C. H. Grandgent's remarks on Dante's allegory in his edition of the poem (revised, 1933), pp. xxxii-xxxiii, where the choice is not made and where allegory and symbolism are lumped together.

5. This, to be sure, is only one of the several arguments that have been adduced in contesting the authenticity of the Letter; but whenever it has been used, it has been taken to bear considerable weight. The most violent attack on the authenticity of the Letter was made by D'Ovidio in an essay entitled "L'Epistola a Cangrande," first published in the *Rivista d'Italia* in 1899 and reprinted in his *Studi sulla Divina Commedia* (1901), in which his remarks on the particular point in question may be taken as typical (*Studi*, pp. 462-463): "Il vero guaio è che l'Epistola soffoca la distinzione tra il senso letterale meramente fittizio, poetico velo d'un concetto allegorico e il senso letterale vero in sè, storico, da cui però o scaturisce una moralità o è raffigurato un fatto soprannaturale. Dei tre efficacissimi esempi danteschi ne dimentica due (Orfeo e i tre Apostoli), e s'attacca al solo terzo, stiracchiandolo per farlo servire anche al senso morale e all'allegorico; nè riuscendo in effetto se non a modulare in tre diverse gradazioni un unico senso niente altro che anagogico. Non è nè palinodia nè plagio; è una parodia. La quale deriva da ciò che, oltre la precisa distinzione tomistica e dantesca del senso allegorico dal morale e dall'anagogico, era in corso la dottrina agostiniana che riduceva tutto alla sola allegoria. Dante ne fa cenno, dove, terminata la definizione del senso allegorico, prosegue: 'Veramente li teologi

questo senso prendono altrimenti che li poeti; ma perocchè mia intenzione è qui lo modo delli poeti seguitare, prenderò il senso allegorico secondo che per li poeti è usato.' Nè, si badi, avrebbe avuto motivo di mutar intenzione, se si fosse posto a chiosar il Paradiso, che, se Dio vuole, è *poesia anch'esso*." [Italics mine]

It is worth noting in this respect that Dr. Edward Moore, in an essay entitled "The Genuineness of the Dedicatory Epistle to Can Grande" (*Studies in Dante,* third series, pp. 284-369) in which he undertook a very careful refutation, point by point, of D'Ovidio's arguments, either did not attribute any importance to the particular objection quoted above or did not see how it was to be met. For a review of the whole dispute, *see* G. Boffito, *L'Epistola di Dante Alighieri a Cangrande della Scala* in *Memorie della R. Acad. delle scienze di Torino,* Series II, vol. 57, of the *Classe di scienze morali,* etc., pp. 5-10.

6. *Opere di Dante* (ed. Società Dantesca Italiana, Florence, 1921), Epistola XIII, 20-25, pp. 438-439.

7. *Summa Theologica,* I, 1, 10. Resp.

8. *De Trinitate,* XV, ix, 15 (PL 43, 1068): "non in verbis sed in facto." On the distinction of the two kinds of allegory in Holy Scripture see *Dictionnaire de théologie catholique* (Vacant, Mangenot, Amann), vol. I (1923), col. 833 ff. s. v. *Allégories bibliques.* On St. Thomas' distinction in particular, consult R. P. P. Synave, "La Doctrine de S. Thomas d'Aquin sur le sens littéral des Écritures" in *Revue Biblique* XXXV (1926), 40-65.

9. "Literal" and "historical" as synonymous terms for the first sense are bound to be puzzling to modern minds. In the discussion of allegory by St. Thomas and others we meet it at every turn. Perhaps no passage can better help us focus our eyes on this concept as they understood it than one in Hugh of St. Victor (cited by Synave, *op. cit.,* p. 43, from Chapter 3 of Hugh's *De scriptoris et scripturibus sacris):* "*Historia* dicitur a verbo graeco ἰστορέω historeo, quod est video et narro; propterea quod apud veteres nulli licebat scribere res gestas, nisi a se visas, ne falsitas admisceretur veritati peccato scriptoris, plus aut minus, aut aliter dicentis. Secundum hoc proprie et districte dicitur historia; sed solet largius accipi ut dicatur historia sensus qui primo loco ex significatione verborum habetur ad res."

10. It may be well to recall on this point that, in St. Thomas' view and that of others, a parable told by Christ has only one sense, namely that *in verbis.* This is true of the Song of Songs, also, and of other parts of Scripture. But in such passages there is no "allegory," because there is no other meaning *in facto.*

11. *Cf.* Thomas Aquinas, *Opuscula selecta* (Paris, 1881) vol. II, pp. 399-401: "Ad quintum dicendum quod quatuor isti sensus non attribuntur sacrae Scripturae, ut in qualibet eius parte sit in istis quatuor sensibus exponenda, sed quandoque istis quatuor, quandoque tribus, quandoque duobus, quandoque unum tantum."

12. Michele Barbi sounded a warning on this matter some years ago, but in so doing appealed to a solution (the poem as "vision," as "apocalypse") which needs I think, further clarification: "Io ho un giorno, durante il positivismo che s'era insinuato nella critica dantesca, richiamato gli studiosi a non trascurare una ricerca così importante come quella del simbolismo nella Divina Commedia: oggi sento il dovere di correre alla difesa del senso

letterale, svilito come azione fittizia, come bella menzogna, quasi che nell'intendimento di Dante l'importanza del suo poema non consista già in quello che egli ha rappresentato nella lettera di esso, ma debba andarsi a cercare in concetti e intendimenti nascosti sotto quella rappresentazione. Non snaturiamo per carità l'opera di Dante; è una rivelazione, non già un'allegoria da capo a fondo. La lettera non è in funzione soltanto di riposti intendimenti, non è bella menzogna: quel viaggio ch'essa descrive è un viaggio voluto da Dio perchè Dante riveli in salute degli uomini quello che ode e vede nel fatale andare." (*Studi danteschi*, I, 12–13.) This is all very well and very much to the point. But the problem which Barbi does not deal with here and which calls for solution is how, on what conceptual basis, is an *allegory* given in a poem in which the first meaning is not a "bella menzogna"?

13. It is essential to remember that I am here concerned with the main allegory of the *Divine Comedy;* otherwise this can appear an oversimplification to any reader familiar with the concrete detail of the poem, and certainly many questions concerning that detail will arise which are not dealt with here. How, for example, are we to explain those passages where the poet urges the reader to look "beneath the veil" for a hidden meaning (*Inferno*, IX, 62; *Purgatorio*, VIII, 19–21)? Do these not point to an "allegory of poets"? I believe that the correct answer can be given in the negative. But, however that may be, we do not meet the main allegory of the poem in such passages.

Likewise, finer distinctions in the allegory of the poem will recognize that the allegory of the opening situation (*Inferno*, I, II) must be distinguished from the main allegory of the poem, and of necessity, since at the beginning the protagonist is still in this life and has not yet begun to move through the world beyond. For some considerations on this point beyond those above in Chapter I, *see* the author's article in RR XXXIX (1948), 269–277: "Sulla fiumana ove'l mar non ha vanto: *Inferno*, II, 108."

14. For a discussion of the absence of allegory in the *Vita Nuova see* the author's *Essay on the Vita Nuova* (Cambridge, Mass., 1948), pp. 110 ff. and *passim.*

15. PL 79, 473. In interpreting the Song of Songs, St. Gregory is not speaking of the kind of allegory which has an historical meaning as its first meaning (*see* note 10 above)—which fact does not make his view of the use of allegory any less interesting or suggestive with respect to Dante's use of it.

16. On created wisdom and the distinction here *see* Augustine, *Confessions*, XII, 15.

17. *Confessions*, VII, 9.

18. *Paradiso*, X, 22–27:

> Or ti riman, lettor, sovra 'l tuo banco,
> dietro pensando a ciò che si preliba,
> s'esser vuoi lieto assai prima che stanco.
> Messo t'ho innanzi: omai per te ti ciba;
> chè a sè torce tutta la mia cura
> quella materia ond'io son fatto scriba.

As every reader of the *Commedia* knows, a poet's voice speaks out frequently in the poem, and most effectively, in various contexts. But these verses may remind us that when the poet does come into the poem, he speaks as scribe, as one remembering and trying to give an adequate account of the event which is now past.

19. Cf. Menendez y Pelayo, *Historia de las ideas estéticas en España,* chapter X, Introduction: "No vino a enseñar estética ni otra ciencia humana el Verbo Encarnado; pero presentò en su persona y en la union de sus dos naturalezas el protótipo más alto de la hermosura, y el objeto más adecuado del amor. . ."

20. Those who refuse to recognize this "mystery" in the allegory of the *Divine Comedy,* who view it instead as the usual "allegory of poets" in which the first meaning is a fiction, are guilty of a reader's error comparable in some way to the error of the Manicheans concerning the Incarnation, as set forth by St. Thomas in the *Summa contra Gentiles,* IV, xxix: "They pretended that whatever He did as man—for instance, that He was born, that He ate, drank, walked, suffered, and was buried—was all unreal, though having some semblance of reality. Consequently they reduced the whole mystery of the Incarnation to a work of fiction."

21. *Comentum* (Florence, 1887), I, 89–90.

22. *Studies in Dante* (second series, 1889), p. 86, n. 1.